READING UNIVERSITY

MEDIEVAL AND RENAISSANCE LATIN TEXTS

THIRTY POEMS
from the
CARMINA BURANA

edited by

P. G. WALSH

University of Glasgow

Published by

Department of Classics, University of Reading

Preface

The Reading University Medieval and Renaissance Latin Texts Series is intended to provide inexpensive annotated texts for use in British Universities.

The requirements of late Latin texts are not necessarily the same as those of classical ones, and are certainly not uniform, so each editor has been left to produce the sort of edition he or she feels suitable for that particular text. The General Editor's role is thus confined to the commissioning, publishing and distribution of texts. Each individual editor is personally solely responsible for his or her interpretation of the text.

A.K. Bate
General Editor

CONTENTS

INTRODUCTION

The <u>Carmina Burana</u> is the popular name given to the poems in the Codex Buranus, a manuscript found in the monastery of Benediktbeuern in Bavaria by Baron von Aretin in 1803, and later transferred to Munich. The main section of the manuscript, copied by three different hands, has been later augmented with compositions which concern us only for the assistance they offer in tracing the history of the manuscript.[1] On this the most distinguished contemporary authority summarises the situation as follows:

"Around 1230 the manuscript was written in a southern border region of the Bavarian-speaking area not far from Italian influence, perhaps in Carinthia, perhaps in Tyrol. Not long afterwards it was connected with a milieu through which the Marner had passed, and the latter's poem for the Provost of Maria Saal would perhaps fix Carinthia as the place of origin.[2] Since the codex seems to have been in the hands of students very soon thereafter, and since a monastic environment seems improbable because of the script, one would think that the manuscript was compiled at the court of a prelate who was a lover of fine books and a patron of students. It follows that Benediktbeuern must definitely be abandoned as its place of origin."[3]

In the original collection of 228 poems we can observe how the three compilers grouped the poems systematically. The first section (1-55) consists of satirical and moralising poems. There follows the second group of love songs and courtly poems which form more than half the collection: these fall into two groups. "In the first group (56-121) the compilers of the <u>Carmina Burana</u> drew considerably on an international repertoire . . . in the second (135-186) they collected a local repertoire, usually adding German stanzas. Between the two comes the curious melange 122-134, which includes songs of Walter of Châtillon and Philip the Chancellor, even lines of Marbod, and only one song (126) that has anything to do with love. One might suppose that the copyists had to return some borrowed non-German manuscript(s) at this stage, and wanted to include all they could before returning it, even if it meant disturbing the overall pattern of the love-songs in their own collection."[4] The third section consists of songs of conviviality and comradeship, with a considerable range of theme and of poetic ability. The original collection concluded with two short plays on religious themes (227-8).

1

All the lyrics were composed to be sung, and in the manuscript nine of the songs[5] as well as one play (227) have the neumes inserted by the same scribe who copied the words. Other hands have inserted melodies for other poems, so that musicologists have now recovered thirty of these tunes.[6] It is probable that the later lyrics which have an additional stanza in German were so written to allow listeners who could not understand the Latin to participate by singing the final stanza.[7] In short, the Carmina Burana is a scholars' song-book.

The three scribes gathered their anthology from several sources. Since the lyrics were sung, many were probably written down from memory, or at the dictation of those who sang them; this would account for the inferior texts of poems whose words are better preserved in other manuscripts. Collections of poems by individuals were probably exploited; one thinks of Omer 351, a manuscript containing 33 poems of Walter of Châtillon and dating from early in the thirteenth century, and the Göttingen manuscript of the Archpoet, as examples of the kind of material available. Then too there was a large number of anthologies of poems by different authors; it is interesting to note how sequences of poems in our manuscript can be paralleled in others.[8] Interestingly enough, music codices are another likely source.[9]

Until recently the only complete edition of the Carmina Burana was that of J.A. Schmeller (Stuttgart 1847). But with the publication in 1970 of the third fascicle of the Heidelberg text begun in 1930 by Hilka and Schumann and now completed by Bischoff, we have a reliable edition of all the poems. A commentary of the first part only (1-55, the moralising and satirical poems) had appeared before Schumann's death, and we still await the continuation of this.

The selection of thirty of the lyrics in this edition attempts to preserve the balance found in the whole collection between the social and convivial poems, the love-lyrics, and the satirical compositions. But the order has been reversed, so that the satirical poems which offer the greatest difficulty of interpretation are placed at the end.

II

Several authors of individual poems in the collection have been identified; they include the Archpoet, Walter of Châtillon, Hugo of Orléans, Philip the Chancellor, and Peter of Blois - all men of learning. Included in this selection are poems by the Archpoet (II) and by Walter of Châtillon (XXV-XXVII); a brief account of these poets will therefore be helpful.

The Archpoet was a German whose real name is unknown. It has been persuasively suggested that he acquired the soubriquet of Archpoet because his patron Rainald Dassel was Archbishop (of Cologne) and Archchancellor of Frederick Barbarossa. The poet, son of a knight, was born about 1130. Nothing is heard of him after the death of his patron in 1167; the emphasis in his poems on his racking cough encourages the speculation that he died young. He lived in the entourage of a patron renowned not only for ecclesiastical and political eminence but also as a classical savant. When Rainald died near Rome, "the news cast its shadow even in Paris; Maecenas was dead." These words of John of Salisbury indicate the conscious cultivation of classical learning by Rainald, who had put pressure on the Archpoet to commemorate in epic verses the Italian campaigns of the emperor. But the Archpoet preferred the less exacting role of a Horace, and in imitation of that model he pleaded that he could not write beyond his powers. Ten of his poems have survived, most in the rhythmical rhyming measures characteristic of medieval lyric; it is the tenth and most famous (Estuans intrinsecus) which appears in the Carmina Burana and accordingly in this selection.[10]

The French poet Walter of Châtillon was perhaps the most learned and certainly the most versatile of the rich crop of twelfth-century poets writing in Latin. Born at Lille about 1135, a student at Paris and Beauvais, and then canon of Reims, he became a member of the circle of John of Salisbury. He was a familiar figure at the court of Henry II of England, whom he attacked bitterly after the murder of Thomas-à-Becket. He eventually settled to a life of teaching at Châtillon, the town whose name he bears. After visits to Bologna and Rome, which provided ammunition for his satirical poetry, he was induced to return to Reims by Archbishop William to become his notary and public orator. His poems mention a leprous condition from which he may have died. Walter was a master of both classical and medieval measures, and inspired a large number of imitators. Of his secular lyrics, his deployment of the pastourelle is particularly attractive. Eventually he renounced erotic composition and confined himself to satire (much of it written for the Feast of Fools) and epic. His Alexandreis, published about 1181 and dedicated to Archbishop William, is an epic written in glorification of Alexander; it is interesting as much for its twelfth-century preoccupation with the perfect man as for its romantic development of the life of Alexander by Curtius.[11]

III

The first six poems in the selection reflect various facets of the life of the twelfth-century scholar about which Helen Waddell has written with such infectious enthusiasm.[12] At the respectable end of these Vagantes we have some of the greatest poets of the age; so the Archpoet travels in the entourage of his Archbishop, and sadly but ironically reflects on his moral lapses when he slips away from his patron's company. At the opposite pole are the rude and rowdy denizens of In taberna (III) or the light-hearted members of the imaginary Order of Wandering Scholars. (I). In all such songs the life and liturgy of the Church is never far away. It is not merely that there is amusing parody of sacred hymns and texts. The gap between Christian ideals and Christian practice is constantly admitted, as in the Archpoet's Confession, or indignantly exposed as in I, where the poet archly claims for his Ordo Vagantum a generosity and a tolerance not always found in the establishments of the regular orders. IV is a splendid example of a begging address, into which names of different dignitaries can be slotted on different occasions. The plaintive claims 'I should like to go to church', 'I should like to work hard' belong to the common stock of such perennial appeals. Omittamus studia (V) takes up a theme familiar in twelfth-century lyrics, the tension between study and sexual inclination, with the 'Gather ye rosebuds', argument thrown in against study. Poem VI has a more original mise-en-scène, an amusing dialogue between brothers, one of whom purposes to enter a monastery. The assembled arguments - appeal from the younger brother, harshness of the monastic regimen, grief of parents - leave the potential monk unmoved. It is only when he is reminded of the parting from his young clerical friend that he changes his mind.

IV

Since the love-lyrics form the largest single group in the collection, they are represented in this edition by seventeen poems (VII-XXIII). Ten of these (VIII-XVII) are shorter lyrics, most of which develop the characteristic motif of the correspondence between the burgeoning of nature in the spring-time and the quickening of love in the poet and his girl. Three poems treat the conventions of courtly love (XVIII-XX), and two are examples of the pastourelle (XXI-XXII). Poem VII is formally a departure-address, but its main theme is the sorrows of love. Finally, XXIII is only loosely attached to this group; though its subject is love, this pastoral dialogue on the merits of cleric and knight as lover is in the tradition of the agon or disputation.

Though one may speak of a conventional structure in VII-XVII (since almost every poem begins with an exultant description of the summer's birth, the glad colours, the happy symphony of spring with which the love-aspirations of the poet seek harmony), there is a fascinating variety of theme within the conventional structure. One lyric concentrates chiefly on the beauties of nature, and adverts to love only in the most incidental way (VIII). Another on the contrary devotes only one stanza to physical nature, and the rest of the poem to the exploration of feelings of love (XI). The normal pattern can be turned on its head; a poem may begin with the sorrows of love which are consoled by the beauty of nature (XIV). As further variation, a poem may be written from the viewpoint of a girl (IX), or of a poet's innocence affected by the first deeper stirrings (XII), or of the poet's experience posing as innocence (X), this last beginning not with the seasons but with the love-life of the classical deities.

The sorrows of love is the commonest theme, and here again the variation is striking. XII represents the static situation of the unacknowledged suitor. In XI the unsuccessful suitor refuses to bow to the situation, and resolves to soldier on. In the memorable originality of <u>Dum Diane</u> (XIII), the night-sky brings relief to the opposed lover. XV explores another dimension of love's sorrows - the pregnancy of the hapless girl. But other poems breathe a happier spirit. XVI is an expression of serene confidence in the fidelity of the poet and of his girl. XVII is a nicely turned piece which begins not with the seasons but with the stars, and fuses astrological lore with the assurance of a happy love-life.

Though it is arbitrary totally to detach 'courtly love' lyrics from the others (for example, XIV has courtly elements), XVIII-XX deserve separate consideration since their themes bear directly on courtly conventions. XVIII is devoted to the theme of malevolent gossip; in the code of courtly love set out by the twelfth-century cleric Andreas Capellanus it is despicable to reveal the affair of another. XIX is a protest about a man's subservience to a proud lady, and demands - ironically, as the final stanza shows - equality between the sexes. XX is set out in the frame of a dream; it is Cupid's lament for the disappearance of Ovid's rules for loving, with emphasis especially on the breaking of confidences, false boasting of conquests, and the usurpation of true love by prostitution or marriage.

The Latin pastourelle, of which XXI-XXII are examples, probably develops out of the vernacular poetry and ultimately out of folk-tradition.[13] In the literature of Provence the poems are already stylised, and the stock variations pass through into the Latin compositions. There is always a <u>locus amoenus</u> - tree providing shade, meadow, stream. The gallant or alternatively the shepherdess loiters there as the other approaches. The heart of the poem lies in the dialogue, as the gallant tries to persuade the girl to linger, and finally imposes his will on her, or alternatively listens to an appeal to his better nature. In the vernacular versions, a wolf is often involved;

the gallant may be promised the girl's hand if he saves her sheep (cf. XXI). The most interesting development in the Latin pastourelle is the deployment of allegory; XXI is introduced by a Christian exordium and becomes a religious poem, a development which occurs also in vernacular poetry.[14]

V

The final poems in the selection (XXIV-XXX) are a melange of satirical poems and moralising pieces. We have already noted that Walter of Châtillon is the author of three of the satirical poems (XXV-XXVII) and XXIV and XXVIII are recognisably in the same tradition. But whereas these last two assail the declining mores of the entire twelfth-century society, Walter's poems are concerned with the avarice of Christians in the Church. So in XXV he berates the various officials of the Roman Curia (making a notable exception of the Pope); in XXVI there is a sadder tone in which he laments the moral decline in both clergy and laity; and in XXVII he repeats this lament, associating the Roman Curia with the clergy at large in the same general charge of simony. The virtues of Walter's poetry stand out for all to see. The firmness of structure, the tenacious and witty exploitation of a central image (the barque of Peter in perilous waters in XXV, hills and valleys representing clergy and laity in XXVI), the effective evocation of classical and Christian literature, the complex yet clear rhyme-schemes, and above all the fondness for effective paradox and oxymoron are the essential features.

The final two poems are moralising pieces. XXIX is the poem which inspired the splendid illustration in the manuscript (which is reproduced in the Hilka-Schumann-Bischoff edition) - Fortune rota volvitur. The poet in learned fashion bewails his fall at the goddess's hands, and generalises the message with the exemplar of Hecuba, widowed and captured at Troy's fall. The final offering is appropriately a prayer for deliverance from the fleeting and delusory pleasures of the world.

VI

The orthography of these poems causes little difficulty. As is well-known, -ae and -oe early developed into -e; in the sixth century Cassiodorus urges his monks when copying: 'A' casui genetivo non subtrahas (Inst. 1 15.9). 'H' occasionally intrudes as in habundas, or disappears as in ortus (= hortus, XXV 28). nichil for nihil, michi for mihi occur frequently.

Looser ablative forms (e.g. molliori, X 2; etheri XII 2) are common in Medieval Latin, sometimes to accommodate a rhyme. The grandiloquent plural used to address a dignitary is found in IV 5-7.

6

The commonest divergences from syntactical norms of Classical Latin are:-

a.   quod + Indic. when the Acc./Inf. construction is found in formal Latin; see XXIII 17, 22, 48; XXI 1. This construction is found in colloquial contexts in Classical Latin, and is especially common in Ecclesiastical Latin.

b.   quod + Indic. to express result = ut + Subj.; e.g. VI 6, XIV 2, XXIII 3 and 4. Note also precor quod . . . pereant (I 3) to express a wish, where Classical Latin might have precor, pereant.

c.   dum + Subj. for temporal cum, as at XX 1, XXI 6, XXIII 1; also for causal cum at IV 5. At XV 16 the Perfect Subj. is merely accommodating the rhyme.

These are the only constructions which need be noted. There are many others which diverge from 'classical' usage but which are often found in prose or poetry from the Augustan period. The ablative of the gerund in a mere participial sense (V 4), forsitan with the Indic. (VI 5, 16), the Inf. of purpose (I 16), the Inf. after dignus (XVIII 1) can all be paralleled in Augustan writers. An expression like satiari exigit (VI 8) is formed by analogy with coronari postulant, a regular classical construction.

It is the vocabulary of some of the poems which makes the Latin less familiar. First, the ecclesiastical words or expressions. Many are of Greek origin - especially when they have a sacramental reference, because the early Christians sought to establish a sacramental language different from that of Roman religion. So, for example, chrisma (XXVII 7), eucharistia (XXVII 3). Other Graecisms have come from Greek through literal translation of the bible; for example, bithalassus (XXV 3), bravium (VIII 5), idolum (XXVII 4); iubileus (XXVI 6) is a Hebraism likewise transmitted. Many of the ecclesiastical words refer to rank, liturgy, administration, or buildings; so clericus, cardinalis, pontifex, pastor; missa, vespera, crucifixus; curia, sanctuarium.

Many medieval usages are attributable to the natural development of the language, parallels for which can be found in Late Latin. unus is often used in the sense of quidam, and parum for paulum; valere is a regular alternative for posse. A long list of words found for the first time in Late Latin could be compiled; e.g. assatura, framea, grossus, impalam, iocundare, leve as adverb, minoratus, modernus, multotiens, principari. Other words originate later: byzantium, cancellaria, decretista, domicella, ferratura, fimbriare, galea = pirate-ship, legista, miles = knight, pastorella, philomena, sterlingus, tena.

Some expressions reflect the influence of the schools, e.g., medium = the mean, secundum quid, absolute, causa/effectus.

7

Notes

1   These consist of Latin songs of the Marner (a 13th Century wandering scholar who composed also in German), a number of hymns, and short verse-dramas on sacred themes; these have been added by about thirty different hands.

2.   Poem 6* is written in praise of Provost Henry of Maria Saal about 1230/1; Maria Saal is north of Klagenfurt.

3.   B.Bischoff, Carmina Burana.   Einführung zur Faksimile Ausgabe der Benediktbeurer Liederhandschrift (Munich 1967). A translation of this Introduction is provided.

4.   So P. Dronke, Medieval Latin and the Rise of European Love-lyric (Oxford 1966), 564.

5.   98-9, 108-9, 119, 128, 131a, 187, 189.

6.   See W. Lipphardt, Die Musik in Geschichte und Gegenwart, 2.853ff., and Arch. f. Musik-Wiss. (1955), 122ff.

7.   There are about 40 of these poems with a German stanza; on their purpose, see H. Spanke, Zeitschr. f. Musik-Wiss. (1931), 246.

8.   Bischoff (n.3) draws attention to a 13th-C. Stuttgart ms. which has nos. 47/47a, 119/120, 131/131a likewise in pairs; cf. also Bodl. Rawlinson C510, containing 14, 15, 19, 21.

9.   Bischoff instances the Florence ms. Laur. Plut. 29.1 (13th C.).

10.   On the Archpoet, see the good edition by Watenphul-Krefeld, Die Gedichte des Archipoeta (Heidelberg 1958); the fullest account in English is in Raby's Secular Latin Poetry II (Oxford 1934), 180ff.

11.   On Walter of Châtillon, see J. de Ghellinck, L'essor de la littérature latine au XIIe siècle (Brussels 1955), 498ff.; Raby, S.L.P. II, 190ff.

12.   Helen Waddell, The Wandering Scholars (London 1927).

13.   See E. Piguet, L'évolution de la pastourelle du XIIe siècle à nos jours (Basle 1927).

14.   See Raby, S.L.P. II 334ff.

8

Abbreviations

Anal. Hymn.	=	Analecta Hymnica Medii Aevi, ed. G.M. Dreves, C. Blunt, H.M. Bannister (Leipzig 1886-1922)
Andreas Capellanus	=	De Amore, ed. P.G. Walsh (London 1982)
CL	=	Classical Latin
Curtius	=	E.R. Curtius, European Literature and the Latin Middle Ages (London 1953)
de Ghellinck	=	J. de Ghellinck, L'essor de la littérature latine au XIIe siècle (Paris 1946)
Dronke	=	P. Dronke, Medieval Latin and The Rise of European Love-lyric 2 vols (Oxford 1965-66)
D.T.C.	=	Dictionnaire de Théologie Catholique
Du Cange	=	Du Cange, Glossarium mediae et infimae Latinitatis
Hilka-Schumann-Bischoff	=	Carmina Burana I 1-3; II 1 (Heidelberg 1930-1970)
Lehmann, Die Parodie	=	P. Lehmann, Die Parodie im Mittelalter (Stuttgart 1963)^2
Par. Texte	=	P. Lehmann, Parodistische Texte (Munich 1923)
Manitius	=	M. Manitius, Geschichte der lateinischen Literatur des Mittelalters (Munich 1911-1931)

ML	=	Medieval Latin
O.B.M.L.V.	=	The Oxford Book of Medieval Latin Verse, ed. F.J.E. Raby
O.D.C.C.	=	Oxford Dictionary of the Christian Church
OF	=	Old French
P.L.	=	Patrologia Latina
Raby, S.L.P.	=	F.J.E. Raby, Secular Latin Poetry 2 vols (Oxford 1934)
R.M.L.W.	=	Revised Medieval Latin Word List, ed. Latham
Southern, W.S.C.M.A.	=	R.W. Southern, Western Society and the Church in the Middle Ages (Harmondsworth 1970)
T.L.L.	=	Thesaurus Linguae Latinae
Walter of Châtillon, Mor.-sat.Ged.	=	Moralisch-satirische Gedichte Walters von Châtillon, ed. Strecker (Heidelberg 1929)
Omer 351	=	Die Lieder Walters von Châtillon in der Handschrift 351 von St. Omer, ed. Strecker (Berlin 1925)
Watenphul-Krefeld	=	H. Watenphul - H. Krefeld, Die Gedichte des Archipoeta (Heidelberg 1958)

I Cum 'in orbem universum' (219)

1.   Cum "in orbem universum" decantatur "ite",
sacerdotes ambulant, currunt cenobite,
et ab evangelio iam surgunt levite,
sectam nostram subeunt, que‾salus est vite.

2.   in secta nostra scriptum est: "Omnia probate!" *Try overly*
vitam nostram optime vos considerate,
contra pravos clericos vos perseverate,
qui non large tribuunt vobis in caritate!

3.   Marchiones, Bawari, Saxones, Australes,
quotquot estis nobiles, vos precor sodales,
auribus percipite novas decretales:
quod avari pereant et non liberales! *Skuflats*

4.   et nos misericordie nunc sumus auctores,
quia nos recipimus magnos et minores;
recipimus et divites et pauperiores,
quos devoti monachi dimittunt extra fores.

5.   nos recipimus monachum cum rasa corona
et si venerit presbyter cum sua matrona,
magistrum cum pueris, virum cum persona,
scolarem libentius tectum veste bona.

6.   secta nostra recipit iustos et iniustos,
claudos atque debiles, <fortes et robustos,
florentes aetatibus> senio onustos,
<frigidos et Veneris ignibus combustos.>

7.   bellosos, pacificos, mites et insanos,
Boëmos, Teutonicos, Sclavos et Romanos,
stature mediocres, gigantes et nanos,
in personis humiles, et econtra vanos.

8.   ordo procul dubio noster secta vocatur
        quam diversi generis populus sectatur:
        ergo 'hic' et 'hec' et 'hoc' ei preponatur,
        quod sit omnis generis qui tot hospitatur.

9.   de vagorum ordine dico vobis iura,
        quorum vita nobilis dulcis est natura,
        quos delectat amplius pinguis assatura,
        severa quam faciat hordei mensura.

10.   ordo noster prohibet matutinas plane.
        sunt quedam phantasmata que vagantur mane,
        per que nobis veniunt visiones vane.
        si quis tunc surrexerit non est mentis sane.

11.   ordo noster prohibet semper matutinas;
        sed statim, cum surgimus, querimus popinas;
        illuc ferri facimus vinum et gallinas;
        nil hic expavescimus preter Hashardi minas.

12.   ordo noster prohibet uti dupla veste;
        tunicam qui recipit ut vadat honeste,
        pallium mox reiicit Decio conteste;
        cingulum huic detrahit ludus manifeste.

13.   quod de summis dicitur in imis teneatur,
        camisia qui fruitur bracis non utatur;
        caliga si sequitur calceus non feratur;
        nam qui hoc transgreditur excommunicatur.

14.   nemo prorsus exeat hospitium ieiunus,
        et, si pauper fuerit, semper petat munus:
        incrementum recipit sepe nummus unus
        cum ad ludum sederit lusor opportunus.

15   nemo in itinere contrarius sit ventis,
                  nec a paupertate ferat vultum condolentis,
                  sed proponat sibi spem semper confidentis.
                  nam post grande malum sors sequitur gaudentis.

16.   ad quos perveneritis, dicatis eis, quare
                  singulorum cupitis mores exprobrare:
                  "Reprobare reprobos et probos probare,
                  et probos ab improbis veni segregare."

II Estuans intrinsecus (191)

1.
Estuans intrinsecus ira vehementi
in amaritudine loquar mee menti:
factus de materia levis elementi
folio sum similis de quo ludunt venti.

2.
cum sit enim proprium viro sapienti
supra petram ponere sedem fundamenti,
stultus ego comparor fluvio labenti
sub eodem aëre nunquam permanenti.

Mtt 7.24

3.
feror ego veluti sine nauta navis,
ut per vias aëris vaga fertur avis.
non me tenent vincula, non me tenet clavis,
quero mei similes et adiungor pravis.

4.
michi cordis gravitas res videtur gravis,
iocus est amabilis dulciorque favis;
quicquid Venus imperat, labor est suavis,
que nunquam in cordibus habitat ignavis.

5.
via lata gradior more iuventutis,
inplico me vitiis immemor virtutis,
voluptatis avidus magis quam salutis,
mortuus in anima curam gero cutis.

7.13

6.
presul discretissime, veniam te precor,
morte bona morior, dulci nece necor;
meum pectus sauciat puellarum decor,
et quas tactu nequeo, saltem corde mechor.

*Reinold Dossel
excellet, just
sweet story*

7.
res est arduissima vincere naturam,
in aspectu virginis mentem esse puram;
iuvenes non possumus legem sequi duram
leviumque corporum non habere curam.

8.   quis in igne positus igne non uratur?
              quis Papie demorans castus habeatur,
              ubi Venus digito iuvenes venatur,
              oculis illaqueat, facie predatur?

9   si ponas Hippolytum hodie Papie,
              non erit Hippolytus in sequenti die:
              Veneris in thalamos ducunt omnes vie,
              non est in tot turribus turris Alethie.

10   secundo redarguor etiam de ludo,
              sed cum ludus corpore me dimittit nudo,
              frigidus exterius mentis estu sudo;
              tunc versus et carmina meliora cudo.

11   tertio capitulo memoro tabernam.
              illam nullo tempore sprevi neque spernam,
              donec sanctos angelos venientes cernam
              cantantes pro mortuis "Requiem eternam".

12   meum est propositum in taberna mori,
              ut sint vina proxima morientis ori.
              tunc cantabunt letius angelorum chori:
              "sit deus propitius huic potatori".

13   poculis accenditur animi lucerna;
              cor inbutum nectare volat ad superna.
              michi sapit dulcius vinum de taberna
              quam quod aqua miscuit presulis pincerna.

14   [loca vitant publica quidam poetarum
              et secretas eligunt sedes latebrarum,
              student instant vigilant nec laborant parum
              et vix tandem reddere possunt opus clarum.

[handwritten annotation: Lke 18.13 / deus propitius esto / michi peccatori]

15   ieiunant et abstinent poetarum chori,
vitant rixas publicas et tumultus fori
et, ut opus faciant quod non possint mori,
moriuntur studio subditi labori.

16   unicuique proprium dat Natura munus:
ego nunquam potui scribere ieiunus;
me ieiunum vincere posset puer unus.
sitim et ieiunium odi tamquam funus.

17   unicuique proprium dat Natura donum:
ego versus faciens bibo vinum bonum
et quod habent purius dolia cauponum;
vinum tale generat copiam sermonum.

18   tales versus facio quale vinum bibo;
nichil possum facere nisi sumpto cibo;
nichil valent penitus que ieiunus scribo;
Nasonem post calicem carmine preibo.

19   michi nunquam spiritus poetrie datur,
nisi prius fuerit venter bene satur;
dum in arce cerebri Bacchus dominatur,
in me Phebus irruit et miranda fatur.]

20   ecce mee proditor pravitatis fui,
de qua me redarguunt servientes tui.
sed eorum nullus est accusator sui,
quamvis velint ludere seculoque frui.

21   iam nunc in presentia presulis beati
secundum dominici regulam mandati
mittat in me lapidem neque parcat vati,
cuius non est animus conscius peccati.

22   sum locutus contra me quicquid de me novi,
      et virus evomui quod tam diu fovi.
      vita vetus displicet, mores placent novi;
      homo videt faciem, sed cor patet Iovi.

23   iam virtutes diligo, vitiis irascor,
      renovatus animo spiritu renascor;
      quasi modo genitus novo lacte pascor,
      ne sit meum amplius vanitatis vas cor.

24   electe Colonie, parce penitenti,
      fac misericordiam veniam petenti
      et da penitentiam culpam confitenti:
      feram quicquid iusseris animo libenti.

25   parcit enim subditis leo rex ferarum
      et est erga subditos immemor irarum,
      et vos idem facite, principes terrarum:
      quod caret dulcedine, nimis est amarum.

III <u>In taberna</u> (196)

1
In taberna quando sumus,
non curamus quid sit humus
sed ad ludum properamus,
cui semper insudamus.
quid agatur in taberna
ubi nummus est pincerna,
hoc est opus ut queratur.
sed quid loquar, audiatur.

2
quidam ludunt, quidam bibunt,
quidam indiscrete vivunt.
sed in ludo qui morantur
ex his quidam denudantur.
quidam ibi vestiuntur,
quidam saccis induuntur.
ibi nullus timet mortem,
sed pro Baccho mittunt sortem.

3
primo pro nummata vini
ex hac bibunt libertini.
semel bibunt pro captivis,
post hec bibunt ter pro vivis,
quater pro Christianis cunctis,
quinquies pro fidelibus defunctis,
sexies pro sororibus vanis,
septies pro militibus silvanis.

4
octies pro fratribus perversis,
novies pro monachis dispersis,
decies pro navigantibus,
undecies pro discordantibus,
duodecies pro penitentibus,
tredecies pro iter agentibus.
tam pro papa quam pro rege
bibunt omnes sine lege.

5
bibit hera, bibit herus,
bibit miles, bibit clerus,
bibit ille, bibit illa,
bibit servus cum ancilla,
bibit velox, bibit piger,
bibit albus, bibit niger,
bibit constans, bibit vagus,
bibit rudis, bibit magus.

6
bibit pauper et egrotus,
bibit exul et ignotus.
bibit puer, bibit canus,
bibit presul et decanus.
bibit soror, bibit frater,
bibit anus, bibit mater.
bibit ista, bibit ille,
bibunt centum, bibunt mille.

7
parum durant sex nummate,
ubi ipsi immoderate
bibunt omnes sine meta,
quamvis bibant mente leta.
sic nos rodunt omnes gentes,
et sic erimus egentes.
qui nos rodunt confundantur,
et cum iustis non scribantur.

1. Exul ego clericus
   ad laborem natus,
   tribulor multotiens
   paupertati datus

4 interesse laudibus
   non possum divinis,
   nec misse nec vespere
   dum cantetur finis.

2 litterarum studiis
   vellem insudare,
   nisi quod inopia
   cogit me cessare.

5 decus, N.
   dum sitis insigne,
   postulo suffragia
   de vobis iam digne.

3 ille meus tenuis
   nimis est amictus;
   sepe frigus patior
   calore relictus

6 ergo mentem capite
   similem Martini,
   vestibus induite
   corpus peregrini,

7 ut vos Deus transferat
   ad regna polorum!
   ibi dona conferat
   vobis beatorum!

V <u>Omittamus studia</u> (75)

1
 Omittamus studia,
  dulce est desipere,
 et carpamus dulcia
  iuventutis tenere!
 res est apta senectuti
  seriis intendere,
 <res est apta iuventuti
  leta mente ludere.>

Refl.
 velox etas praeterit
  studio detenta
 lascivire suggerit
  tenera iuventa.

2
 ver etatis labitur,
  hiems nostra properat,
 vita damnum patitur
  cura carnem macerat.
 sanguis aret, hebet pectus,
  minuuntur gaudia,
 nos deterret iam senectus
  morborum familia.

Refl.

3
 imitemur superos!
  digna est sententia,
 et amores teneros
  iam venentur retia.
 voto nostro serviamus!
  mos est iste numinum.
 ad plateas descendamus
  et choreas virginum!

Refl.

4
 ibi, que fit facilis,
  est videndi copia,
 ibi fulget mobilis
  membrorum lascivia.
 dum puelle se movendo
  gestibus lasciviunt,
 asto videns, et videndo
  me michi subripiunt.

Refl.

1 "Deus pater, adiuva,
quia mors est proxima!
si concedis crastinum,
faciam me monachum.

2 festina succurrere!
iam me vult invadere!
dona, pater, spatium,
da michi consilium!"

3 "O mi dilectissime,
quidnam cupis agere?
secus tibi consule,
noli me relinquere!"

4 "Tua, frater, pietas
movet michi lacrimas,
quia eris orphanus,
postquam ero monachus."

5 "Ergo mane paululum
saltim post hoc triduum!
forsan hoc periculum
non erit mortiferum."

6 "Tanta est angustia,
que currit per viscera,
quod est michi dubia
vita quoque crastina."

7 "Monachilis regula
non est tibi cognita?
ieiunant cottidie,
vigilant assidue."

9 "Dura donat pabula,
fabas ac legumina,
post tale convivium
potum aque modicum."

10 "Quid prosunt convivia
quidve Dionysia,
ubi et de dapibus
caro datur vermibus?"

11 "Vel parentum gemitus
moveat te penitus,
qui te plangit monachum
velut vita mortuum."

12 "Qui parentes diligit
atque Deum negligit,
reus inde fuerit,
quando iudex venerit."

13 "O ars dialectica,
numquam esses cognita,
que tot facis clericos
exules ac miseros!

14 numquam magis videris,
quem tu tantum diligis:
illum parvum clericum
N. pulcherrimum."

15 "Hëu michi misero!
quid faciam, nescio,
longo in exilio.
sum sine consilio.

8   "Qui pro Deo vigilant,   16   parce, frater, fletibus!
      coronari postulant;   forsitan fit melius.
      qui pro Deo esurit,   iam mutatur animus:
      satiari exigit."   nondum ero monachus."

VII <u>Dulce solum</u> (119)

1   Dulce solum   natalis patrie,
    domus ioci,   thalamus gratie,
    vos relinquam   aut cras aut hodie,
    periturus   amoris rabie.

2   vale tellus,   valete socii,
    quos benigno   favore colui,
    et me dulcis   consortem studii
    deplangite,   qui vobis perii!

3   igne novo   Veneris saucia
    mens, que prius   non novit talia,
    nunc fatetur   vera proverbia:
    "ubi amor,   ibi miseria."

4   quot sunt apes   in Hyble vallibus,
    quot vestitur   Dodona frondibus
    et quot natant   pisces equoribus,
    tot abundat   amor doloribus.

VIII <u>Letabundus rediit</u> (74)

1   Letabundus rediit
    avium concentus,
    ver iocundum prodiit,
    gaudeat iuventus
    nova ferens gaudia;
    modo vernant omnia,
    Phebus serenatur,
    redolens temperiem
    novo flore faciem
    Flora renovatur.

2   risu Iovis pellitur
    torpor hiemalis,
    altius extollitur
    cursus estivalis
    solis, beneficio
    <cuius omnis regio>
    recipit teporem.
    sic ad instar temporis
    nostri Venus pectoris
    reficit ardorem.

3   estivantur Dryades
    colle sub umbroso,
    prodeunt Oreades
    cetu glorioso,
    Satyrorum contio
    psallit cum tripudio
    Tempe per amena;
    his alludens concinit
    cum iocundi meminit
    veris philomena.

4   estas ab exilio
    redit exoptata,
    picto redit gremio
    tellus purpurata.
    miti cum susurrio
    suo domicilio
    gryllus delectatur;
    hoc canore, iubilo,
    multiformi sibilo
    nemus gloriatur.

5   applaudamus igitur
    rerum novitati,
    felix, qui diligitur
    voti compos grati,
    dono letus Veneris,
    cuius ara teneris
    floribus odorat.
    miser e contrario
    qui sublato bravio
    sine spe laborat.

IX <u>Tempus adest floridum</u> (142)

1   Tempus adest floridum,   surgunt namque flores,
     vernales [mox] in omnibus   immutantur mores.
     hoc, quod frigus leserat,   reparant calores;
     cernimus hoc fieri   per multos colores.

2   stant prata plena floribus,   in quibus nos ludamus!
     virgines cum clericis   simul procedamus,
     per amorem Veneris   ludum faciamus,
     ceteris virginibus   ut hoc referamus!

3   "O dilecta domina,   cur sic alienaris?
     an nescis, o carissima,   quod sic adamaris?
     si tu esses Helena,   vellem esse Paris!
     tamen potest fieri   noster amor talis."

X Amor habet (88)

1   Amor habet superos;
        Iovem amat Iuno;
     motus premens efferos
        imperat Neptuno;
     Pluto tenens inferos
        mitis est hoc uno.

Refl.   amoris solamine
     virgino cum virgine;
     aro non in semine,
     pecco sine crimine.

2   amor trahit teneros
        molliori nexu,
     rigidos et asperos
        duro frangit flexu;
     capitur rhinoceros
        virginis amplexu.

Refl.

3   virgo cum virginibus
        horreo corruptas,
     et cum meretricibus
        simul odi nuptas;
     nam in istis talibus
        turpis est voluptas.

Refl.

4   virginis egregie
        ignibus calesco
     et eius cotidie
        in amore cresco;
     sol est in meridie,
        nec ego tepesco.

Refl.

5   gratus super omnia
        ludus est puelle,
     et eius precordia
        omni carent felle;
     sunt que prestat basia
        dulciora melle.

Refl.

6   ludo cum Cecilia
        nichil timeatis!
     sum quasi custodia
        fragilis etatis,
     ne marcescant lilia
        sue castitatis.

Refl.

7   flos est; florem tangere
       non est res secura.
    uvam sino crescere
       donec sit matura;
    spes me facit vivere
       letum re ventura.

8   volo tantum ludere,
       id est, contemplari,
    presens loqui, tangere,
       tandem osculari;
    quintum, quod est agere,
       noli suspicari!

Refl.   Refl.

9   quidquid agant ceteri,
       virgo, sic agamus,
    ut, quem decet fieri,
       ludum faciamus;
    ambo sumus teneri;
       tenere ludamus!

Refl.

1   Transit nix et glacies
    spirante Favonio
    terre nitet facies
    ortu florum vario;
    et michi materies
    amor est, quem sentio.

Refl.   ad gaudia
            temporis nos ammonet
                lascivia.

2   agnosco vestigia
    rursus flamme veteris;
    planctus et suspiria
    nove signa Veneris,
    a quo monet tristia
    amantes pre ceteris.

Refl.

3   illa, pro qua gravior
    mens amorem patitur,
    iusto plus asperior
    nec michi compatitur.
    amans, et non mentior,
    nec vivit nec moritur.

Refl.

4   hic amor, hic odium;
    quid eligam, nescio.
    sic feror in dubium,
    sed cum hanc respicio,
    me furatur inscium
    et prorsus deficio.

Refl.

5   non est finis precibus,
    quamvis cantu finiam;
    superis faventibus
    adhuc illi serviam,
    unde letis plausibus
    optata percipiam!
        Refl.

XII <u>Tempus accedit floridum</u> (114)

1   Tempus accedit floridum
    hiems discedit temere;
    omne, quod fuit aridum,
    germen suum vult gignere.
    quamdiu modo vixeris,
semper letare, iuvenis   quia nescis, cum deperis!

2   prata iam rident omnia,
    est dulce flores carpere;
    sed nox donat his somnia,
    qui semper vellent ludere.
    ve, ve, miser quid faciam?
Venus, michi subvenias!   tuam iam colo gratiam.

3   plangit cor meum misere,
    quia caret solacio;
    si velles, hoc cognoscere
    bene posses, ut sentio.
    o tu virgo pulcherrima,
si non audis me miserum,   michi mors est asperrima!

4   dulcis appares omnibus,
    sed es michi dulcissima:
    tu pre cunctis virginibus
    incedis ut castissima.
    ✝ o tu mitis considera!
✝ nam pro te gemitus   passus sum et suspiria.

1   Dum Diane vitrea
    sero lampas oritur,
    et a fratris rosea
    luce dum succenditur,
    dulcis aura Zephyri
    spirans omnes etheri
    nubes tollit;
    sic emollit
    vi chordarum pectora,
    et immutat
    cor, quod nutat
    ad amoris pondera.

2   letum iubar Hesperi
    gratiorem
    dat humorem
    roris soporiferi
    mortalium generi.

3   o quam felix est antidotum soporis!
    quot curarum tempestates sedat et doloris!
        dum surrepit clausis oculorum poris,
    ipsum gaudio equiperat dulcedini amoris.

4   Morpheus in mentem
    trahit impellentem
    ventum lenem segetes maturas,
    murmura rivorum per harenas puras,
    circulares ambitus molendin⟨ari⟩orum
    qui furantur somno lumen oculorum.

XIV O comes amoris, dolor (111)

1 O comes amoris, dolor,
   cuius mala male solor,
     an habes remedium?
   dolor urget me, nec mirum,
   quem a predilecta dirum,
     en, vocat exilium.
   cuius laus est singularis
   pro qua non curasset Paris
     Helene consortium.

2 sed quid queror me remotum
   illi fore, que devotum
     me fastidit hominem,
   cuius nomen tam verendum
   quod nec michi presumendum
     est, ut eam nominem?
   ob quam causam mei mali
   me frequenter vultu tali
     respicit quo neminem?

3 ergo solus solam amo,
   cuius captus sum ab hamo
     nec vicem reciprocat.
   quam enutrit vallis quedam
   quam ut paradisum credam
     in qua pius collocat
   hanc creator creaturam
   vultu claram, mente puram,
     quam cor meum invocat.

4 gaude, vallis insignita,
   vallis rosis redimita,
     vallis, flos convallium,
   inter valles vallis una
   quam collaudat sol et luna
     dulcis cantus avium!
   te collaudat philomena
   vallis dulcis et amena,
     mestis dans solacium!

1   Huc usque, me miseram!
rem bene celaveram
et amavi callide.

2   res mea tandem patuit
nam venter intumuit,
partus instat gravide.

3   hinc mater me verberat,
hinc pater improperat,
ambo tractant aspere.

4   sola domi sedeo,
egredi non audeo
nec inpalam ludere.

5   cum foris egredior,
a cunctis inspicior,
quasi monstrum fuerim.

6   cum vident hunc uterum,
alter pulsat alterum,
silent dum transierim.

7   semper pulsant cubito
me designant digito
ac si mirum fecerim.

8   nutibus me indicant
dignam rogo iudicant
quod semel peccaverim.

9   quid percurram singula?
ego sum in fabula
et in ore omnium.

10   ex eo vim patior
iam dolore morior
semper sum in lacrimis.

11   hoc dolorem cumulat
quod amicus exulat
propter illud paululum.

12   ob patris sevitiam
recessit in Franciam
a finibus ultimis.

13   \<iam\> sum in tristitia
de eius absentia
in doloris cumulum.

XVI Omnia sol temperat (136)

1 Omnia sol temperat,
　　purus et subtilis,
novo mundo reserat
　　faciem Aprilis;
ad amorem properat
　　animus herilis,
et iocundis imperat
　　deus puerilis.

2 　rerum tanta novitas
　　　in sollemni vere
　　et veris auctoritas
　　　iubet nos gaudere.
　　vices prebet solitas;
　　　et in tuo vere,
　　fides est et probitas
　　　tuum retinere.

3 　ama me fideliter!
　　　fidem meam nota:
　de corde totaliter
　　　et ex mente tota
　sum presentialiter
　　　absens in remota.
　quisquis amat aliter
　　　volvitur in rota.

33

XVII Iove cum Mercurio (88a)

1 Iove cum Mercurio   Geminos tenente
   et a Libra Venere   Martem expellente
   virgo nostra nascitur,   Tauro tunc latente.

2 natus ego pariter   sub eisdem signis
   pari par coniunctus sum   legibus benignis:
   paribus est ignibus   par accensus ignis.

3 solus solam diligo   sic me sola solum,
   nec est cui liceat   immiscere dolum;
   non in vanum variant   signa nostra polum.

4 obicit "ab alio"   forsitan "amatur"
   ut quod "solus" dixerim,   ita refellatur;
   sed ut dictum maneat,   sic determinatur.

1 Lingua mendax et dolosa,
   lingua procax, venenosa,
   lingua digna detruncari
   et in igne concremari,

2 que me dicit deceptorem
   et non fidum amatorem,
   quam amabam, dimisisse
   et ad alteram transisse!

3 sciat deus, sciant dei:
   non sum reus huius rei!
   sciant dei, sciat deus:
   huius rei non sum reus!

4 unde iuro Musas novem
   quod et maius est, per Iovem,
   qui pro Dane sumpsit auri,
   in Europa formam tauri;

5 iuro Phebum, iuro Martem,
   qui amoris sciant artem;
   iuro quoque te, Cupido,
   arcum cuius reformido;

6 arcum iuro cum sagittis
   quas frequenter in me mittis:
   sine fraude, sine dolo
   fedus hoc servare volo!

7 volo fedus observare
   et ad hec dicemus, quare:
   inter choros puellarum
   nichil vidi tam preclarum.

8 inter quas appares ita
   ut in auro margarita.
   humeri, pectus et venter
   sunt formata tam decenter.

9 frons et gula, labra, mentum
   dant amoris alimentum;
   crines eius adamavi
   quoniam fuere flavi.

10 ergo dum nox erit dies,
   et dum labor erit quies,
   et dum aqua erit ignis,
   et dum silva sine lignis,

11 et dum mare sine velis
   et dum Parthus sine telis,
   cara michi semper eris,
   nisi fallar, non falleris!

XIX Volo virum vivere viriliter (178)

1 Volo virum vivere   viriliter;
   diligam si diligar   equaliter;
   sic amandum censeo,   non aliter.
   hac in parte fortior   quam Iupiter
      nescio procari
      commercio vulgari:
   amaturus forsitan,   volo prius amari.

2 muliebris animi   superbiam
   gravi supercilio   despiciam,
   nec maiorem terminum   subiciam
   neque bubus aratrum   preficiam.
      displicet hic usus
      in miseros diffusus
   malo plaudens ludere   quam plangere delusus.

3 que cupit, ut placeat,   huic placeam;
   ipsa prior faveat,   ut faveam.
   non ludemus aliter   hanc aleam,
   ne se granum reputet   me paleam.
      pari lege fori
      deserviam amori,
   ne prosternar impudens   femineo pudori.

4 liber ego liberum   me iactito,
   casto pene similis   Hippolyto,
   nec me vincit mulier   tam subito
   que seducat oculis   ac digito.
      dicat me placere
      et diligat sincere;
   hec michi protervitas   placet in muliere.

36

5 ecce michi displicet,   quod cecini,

 et meo contrarius   sum carmini,

 tue reus, domina,   dulcedini,

 cuius elegantie   non memini.

  quia sic erravi

  sum dignus pena gravi;

 penitentem corripe,   si placet in conclavi.

XX Dum curata vegetarem (105)

1   Dum curata vegetarem
    soporique membra darem,
    et langueret animalis
    prevaleret naturalis
      virtutis dominium,

2   en Cupido pharetratus
    crinali torque spoliatus,
    manu multa tactis alis,
    mesto vultu, numquam talis,
    visus est per somnium.

3   quem ut vidi perturbatum
    habituque disturbatum
    membra stupor ingens pressit.
    qui paulatim ut recessit
    a membris organicis,

4   causam quero mesti vultus
    et sic deformati cultus,
    cur sint ale contrectate
    nec ut decet ordinate,
      causam et itineris.

5   Amor, quondam vultu suavis
    nunc merore gravi gravis
    ut me vidit percunctari
    responsumque prestolari
    reddit causam singulis:

6   "vertitur in luctum organum Amoris,
    canticum subductum absinthio doloris,
    vigor priscus abiit, evanuit iam virtus.
    me vis deseruit, periere Cupidinis arcus!

7   artes amatorie iam non instruuntur,
    a Nasone tradite passim pervertuntur;
    nam siquis istis utitur, more modernorum
    turpiter Tabutitur hac assuetudine morum.

8   Naso, meis artibus et regulis instructus
    mundique voluptatibus feliciter subductus,
    ab errore studuit mundum revocare;
    qui sibi notus erat, docuit sapienter amare.

9   Veneris mysteria iam non occultantur
    cistis, sed exposita coram presentantur.
    proh dolor! non dedecet palam commisceri?
    precipue Cytherea iubet sua sacra taceri.

10   amoris ob infamiam moderni gloriantur,
    sine re iactantiam anxii venantur,
    iactantes sacra Veneris corporibus non tactis.
    eheu, nocturnis titulos imponimus actis!

11   res arcana Veneris virtutibus habenda
    optimisque meritis et moribus emenda,
    prostat in prostibulo, redigitur in pactum;
    tanta meum populo ius est ad damna redactum."

XXI Lucis orto sidere (157)

1   Lucis orto sidere
    exit virgo propere
      facie vernali,
    oves iussa regere
      baculo pastorali.

2   sol effundens radium
    dat calorem nimium.
      virgo speciosa
    solem vitat noxium
      sub arbore frondosa.

3   dum procedo paululum,
    lingue solvo vinculum:
      "salve, rege digna!
    audi, queso, servulum,
      esto michi benigna!"

4   "cur salutas virginem
    que non novit hominem,
      ex quo fuit nata?
    sciat Deus! neminem
      inveni per hec prata."

5   forte lupus aderat,
    quem fames expulerat
      gutturis avari.
    ove rapta properat
      cupiens saturari.

6   dum puella cerneret,
    quod sic ovem perderet,
      pleno clamat ore:
    "si quis ovem redderet
      me gaudeat uxore!"

7   mox ut vocem audio,
    denudato gladio
      lupus immolatur,
    ovis ab exitio
      redempta reportatur.

XXII Estivali sub fervore (79)

1 Estivali sub fervore
quando cuncta sunt in flore,
totus eram in ardore,
sub olive me decore,
estu fessum et sudore,
detinebat mora.

2 erat arbor hec in prato
quovis flore picturato,
herba, fonte, situ grato,
sed et umbra, flatu dato.
stilo non pinxisset Plato
loca gratiora.

3 subest fons vivacis vene
adest cantus philomene
Naiadumque cantilene.
paradisus hic est pene:
non sunt loca, scio plene,
his iocundiora.

4 hic dum placet delectari
delectatque iocundari
et ab estu relevari,
cerno forma singulari
pastorellam sine pari
colligentem mora.

5 in amorem vise cedo;
fecit Venus hoc, ut credo.
"ades" inquam "non sum predo,
nichil tollo, nichil ledo.
me meaque tibi dedo
pulchrior quam Flora!"

6 que respondit verbo brevi:
"ludos viri non assuevi.
sunt parentes michi sevi:
mater longioris evi
irascetur pro re levi.
parce nunc in hora."

XXIII Anni parte florida (92)

1   Anni parte florida,   celo puriore,
    picto terre gremio   vario colore,
    dum fugaret sidera   nuntius Aurore,
    liquit somnus oculos   Phyllidis et Flore.

2   placuit virginibus   ire spatiatum,
    nam soporem reicit   pectus sauciatum;
    equis ergo passibus   exeunt in pratum,
    ut et locus faciat   ludum esse gratum.

3   eunt ambe virgines   et ambe regine,
    Phyllis coma libera,   Flore compto crine.
    non sunt forme virginum,   sed forme divine,
    et respondent facies   luci matutine.

4   nec stirpe nec facie   nec ornatu viles
    et annos et animos   habent iuveniles;
    sed sunt parum impares   et parum hostiles,
    nam huic placet clericus   et huic placet miles.

5   non eis distantia   corporis aut oris,
    omnia communia   sunt intus et foris,
    sunt unius habitus   et unius moris;
    sola differentia   modus est amoris.

6   susurrabat modicum   ventus tempestivus,
    locus erat viridi   gramine festivus,
    et in ipso gramine   defluebat rivus
    vivus atque garrulo   murmure lascivus.

7   ad augmentum decoris   et caloris minus
    fuit secus rivulum   spatiosa pinus,
    venustata folio,   late pandens sinus,
    nec intrare poterat   calor peregrinus.

41

8 consedere virgines;   herba sedem dedit.
   Phyllis iuxta rivulum, Flora longe sedit.
   et dum sedet utraque,   dum in sese redit,
   amor corda vulnerat   et utramque ledit.

9 amor est interius   latens et occultus
   et corde certissimos   elicit singultus;
   pallor genas inficit,   alternantur vultus,
   sed in verecundia   furor est sepultus.

10 Phyllis in suspirio   Floram deprehendit,
   et hanc de consimili   Flora reprehendit;
   altera sic alteri   mutuo rependit;
   tandem morbum detegit   et vulnus ostendit.

11 ille sermo mutuus   multum habet more,
   et est quidem series   tota de amore;
   amor est in animis,   amor est in ore.
   tandem Phyllis incipit et arridet Flore.

12 "miles", inquit, "inclite, mea cura, Paris!
   ubi modo militas   et ubi moraris?
   o vita militie,   vita singularis,
   sola digna gaudio   Dionei laris!"

13 dum puella militem   recolit amicum,
   Flora ridens oculos   iacit in obliquum
   et in risu loquitur   verbum inimicum:
   "amas", inquit, "poteras dicere, mendicum.

14 sed quid Alcibiades   facit, mea cura,
   res creata dignior   omni creatura,
   quem beavit omnibus   gratiis Natura?
   o sola felicia   clericorum iura!"

15 Floram Phyllis arguit   de sermone duro
    et sermone loquitur   Floram commoturo;
    nam "ecce virgunculam"   inquit "corde puro,
    cuius pectus nobile   servit Epicuro!

16 surge, surge, misera,   de furore fedo!
    solum esse clericum   Epicurum credo;
    nichil elegantie   clerico concedo,
    cuius implet latera   moles et pinguedo.

17 a castris Cupidinis   cor habet remotum
    qui somnum desiderat   et cibum et potum.
    o puella nobilis,   omnibus est notum,
    quod est longe militis   ab hoc voto votum.

18 solis necessariis   miles est contentus,
    somno, cibo, potui   non vivit intentus;
    amor illi prohibet,   ne sit somnolentus,
    cibus, potus militis   amor et iuventus.

19 quis amicos copulet   nostros loro pari?
    lex, natura sineret   illos copulari?
    meus novit ludere,   tuus epulari;
    meo semper proprium   dare, tuo dari."

20 haurit Flora sanguinem   vultu verecundo
    et apparet pulchrior   in risu secundo,
    et tandem eloquio   reserat facundo,
    quod corde conceperat   artibus fecundo.

21 "satis", inquit, "libere,   Phyllis, es locuta,
    multum es eloquio   velox et acuta,
    sed non efficaciter   verum prosecuta,
    ut per te prevaleat   lilio cicuta.

22 dixisti de clerico,   quod indulget sibi,
    servum somni nominas   et potus et cibi.
    sic solet ab invido   probitas describi;
    ecce, parum patere,   respondebo tibi.

23 tot et tanta, fateor,   sunt amici mei,
    quod numquam incogitat   aliene rei.
    celle mellis, olei,   Cereris, Lyei,
    aurum, gemme, pocula   famulantur ei.

24 in tam dulci copia   vite clericalis,
    quod non potest aliqua   pingi voce talis,
    volat et duplicibus   Amor plaudit alis,
    Amor indeficiens,   Amor immortalis.

25 sentit tela Veneris   et Amoris ictus,
    non est tamen clericus   macer aut afflictus,
    quippe nulla gaudii   parte derelictus;
    cui respondet animus   domine non fictus.

26 macer est et pallidus   tuus preelectus,
    pauper et vix pallio   sine pelle tectus,
    non sunt artus validi   nec robustum pectus;
    nam cum causa deficit,   deest et effectus.

27 turpis est pauperies   imminens amanti.
    quid prestare poterit   miles postulanti?
    sed dat multa clericus   et ex abundanti;
    tante sunt divitie   reditusque tanti."

28 Flore Phyllis obicit: "multum es perita
    in utrisque studiis   et utraque vita,
    satis probabiliter   et pulchre mentita;
    sed hec altercatio   non quiescet ita.

29	cum orbem letificat	hora lucis feste,
	tunc apparet clericus	satis inhoneste,
	in tonsura capitis	et in atra veste
	portans testimonium	voluptatis meste.

29 cum orbem letificat hora lucis feste,
    tunc apparet clericus satis inhoneste,
    in tonsura capitis et in atra veste
    portans testimonium voluptatis meste.

30 non est ullus adeo fatuus aut cecus,
    cui non appareat militare decus.
    tuus est in otio quasi brutum pecus;
    meum terit galea, meum portat equus.

31 meus armis dissipat inimicas sedes,
    et si forte prelium solus init pedes,
    dum tenet Bucephalam suus Ganymedes,
    ille me commemorat inter ipsas cedes.

32 redit fusis hostibus et pugna confecta
    et me sepe respicit galea reiecta.
    ex his et ex aliis ratione recta
    est vita militie michi preelecta."

33 novit iram Phyllidis et pectus anhelum
    et remittit multiplex illi Flora telum.
    "frustra", dixit, "loqueris os ponens in celum,
    et per acum niteris figere camelum.

34 mel pro felle deseris et pro falso verum,
    que probas militiam reprobando clerum.
    facit amor militem strenuum et ferum?
    non! immo pauperies et defectus rerum.

35 pulchra Phyllis, utinam sapienter ames
    nec veris sententiis amplius reclames!
    tuum domat militem et sitis et fames,
    quibus mortis petitur et inferni trames.

36   multum est calamitas   militis attrita,
       sors illius dura est   et in arto sita,
       cuius est in pendulo   dubioque vita,
       ut habere valeat   vite requisita.

37   non dicas opprobrium,   si cognoscas morem,
       vestem nigram clerici,   comam breviorem:
       habet ista clericus   ad summum honorem,
       ut sese significet   omnibus maiorem.

38   universa clerico   constat esse prona,
       et signum imperii   portat in corona.
       imperat militibus   et largitur dona:
       famulante maior est   imperans persona.

39   otiosum clericum   semper esse iuras:
       viles spernit operas,   fateor, et duras;
       sed cum eius animus   evolat ad curas,
       celi vias dividit   et rerum naturas.

40   meus est in purpura,   tuus in lorica;
       tuus est in prelio,   meus in lectica,
       ubi gesta principum   relegit antiqua,
       scribit, querit, cogitat   totum de amica.

41   quid Dione valeat   et amoris deus,
       primus novit clericus   et instruxit meus;
       factus est per clericum   miles Cythereus,
       his est et huiusmodi   tuus sermo reus."

42   liquit Flora pariter   vocem et certamen
       et sibi Cupidinis   exigit examen,
       Phyllis primum obstrepit,   acquiescit tamen,
       et probato iudice   redeunt per gramen.

43 totum in Cupidine   certamen est situm;
    suum dicunt iudicem   verum et peritum,
    quia vite noverit   utriusque ritum;
    et iam sese preparant,   ut eant auditum.

44 pari forma virgines   et pari pudore,
    pari voto militant   et pari colore:
    Phyllis veste candida,   Flora bicolore;
    mulus vector Phyllidis   erat, equus Flore.

45 mulus quidem Phyllidis   mulus erat unus,
    quem creavit, aluit,   domuit Neptunus.
    hunc post apri rabiem,   post Adonis funus
    misit pro solacio   Cytheree munus.

46 pulchre matri Phyllidis et probe regine
    illum tandem prebuit   Venus Hiberine,
    eo quod indulserat   opere divine;
    ecce Phyllis possidet   illum leto fine.

47 faciebat nimium   virginis persone:
    pulcher erat, habilis   et stature bone,
    qualem esse decuit,   quem a regione
    tam longinqua miserat   Nereus Dione.

48 qui de superpositis   et de freno querunt,
    quod totum argenteum   dentes muli terunt,
    sciant, quod hec omnia   talia fuerunt,
    qualia Neptunium   munus decuerunt.

49 non decore caruit   illa Phyllis hora,
    sed multum apparuit   dives et decora;
    et non minus habuit   utriusque Flora,
    nam equi predivitis   freno domat ora.

50   equus ille, domitus   Pegaseis loris,
        multum pulchritudinis   habet et valoris,
        pictus artificio   varii coloris;
        nam mixtus nigredini   color est oloris.

51   forme fuit habilis,   etatis primeve,
        et respexit paululum   tumide, non seve;
        cervix fuit ardua,   coma sparsa leve,
        auris parva, prominens   pectus, caput breve.

52   dorso pando iacuit   virgini sessure
        spina, que non senserat   aliquid pressure.
        pede cavo, tibia   recta, largo crure,
        totum fuit sonipes   studium Nature.

53   equo superposita   radiabat sella;
        ebur enim medium   clausit auri cella,
        et, cum essent quattuor   selle capitella,
        venustavit singulum   gemma quasi stella.

54   multa de preteritis   rebus et ignotis
        erant mirabilibus   ibi sculpta notis;
        nuptie Mercurii   superis admotis,
        fedus, matrimonium,   plenitudo dotis.

55   nullus ibi locus est   vacuus aut planus;
        habet plus, quam capiat   animus humanus.
        solus illa sculpserat,   que spectans Vulcanus
        vix hoc suas credidit   potuisse manus.

56   pretermisso clipeo   Mulciber Achillis
        laboravit phaleras   et indulsit illis;
        ferraturam pedibus   et frenum maxillis
        et habenas addidit   de sponse capillis.

57	sellam texit purpura	subinsuta bysso,
	quam Minerva, reliquo	studio dimisso,
	acantho texuerat	et flore narcisso
	et per tenas margine	fimbriavit scisso.

58	volant equis pariter	due domicelle;
	vultus verecundi sunt	et gene tenelle.
	sic emergunt lilia,	sic rose novelle,
	sic decurrunt pariter	due celo stelle.

59	ad Amoris destinant	ire paradisum.
	dulcis ira commovet	utriusque visum;
	Phyllis Flore, Phyllidi	Flora movet risum.
	fert Phyllis accipitrem	manu, Flora nisum.

60	parvo tractu temporis	nemus est inventum.
	ad ingressum nemoris	murmurat fluentum,
	ventus inde redolet	myrrham et pigmentum,
	audiuntur tympana	cithareque centum.

61	quicquid potest hominum	comprehendi mente,
	totum ibi virgines	audiunt repente:
	vocum differentie	sunt illic invente,
	sonat diatessaron,	sonat diapente.

62	sonant et mirabili	plaudunt harmonia
	tympanum, psalterium,	lyra, symphonia,
	sonant ibi phiale	voce valde pia,
	et buxus multiplici	cantum prodit via.

63	sonant omnes avium	lingue voce plena:
	vox auditur merule	dulcis et amena,
	corydalus, graculus	atque philomena,
	que non cessat conqueri	de transacta pena.

64	instrumento musico,	vocibus canoris,
	tunc diversi specie	contemplata floris,
	tunc odoris gratia	redundante foris
	coniectatur teneri	thalamus Amoris.

65	virgines introeunt	modico timore
	et eundo propius	crescunt in amore.
	sonat queque volucrum	proprio rumore,
	accenduntur animi	vario clamore.

66	immortalis fieret	ibi manens homo.
	arbor ibi quelibet	suo gaudet pomo,
	vie myrrha, cinnamo	fraglant et amomo;
	coniectari poterat	dominus ex domo.

67	vident choros iuvenum	et domicellarum,
	singulorum corpora	corpora stellarum.
	capiuntur subito	corda puellarum
	in tanto miraculo	rerum novellarum.

68	sistunt equos pariter	et descendunt, pene
	oblite propositi	sono cantilene.
	sed auditur iterum	cantus philomene,
	et statim virginee	recalescunt vene.

69	circa silve medium	locus est occultus,
	ubi viget maxime	suus deo cultus:
	Fauni, Nymphe, Satyri,	comitatus multus
	tympanizant, concinunt	ante dei vultus.

70	portant vina manibus	et coronas florum;
	Bacchus Nymphas instruit	et choros Faunorum.
	servant pedum ordinem	et instrumentorum;
	sed Silenus titubat	nec psallit in chorum.

71   somno vergit senior   asino prevectus
        et in risus copiam   solvit dei pectus.
        clamat "vina!" remanet   clamor imperfectus:
        viam vocis impedit   vinum et senectus.

72   inter hec aspicitur   Cytheree natus:
        vultus est sidereus,   vertex est pennatus,
        arcum leva possidet   et sagittas latus;
        satis potest conici   potens et elatus.

73   sceptro puer nititur   floribus perplexo,
        stillat odor nectaris   de capillo pexo.
        tres assistunt Gratie   digito connexo
        et amoris calicem   tenent genu flexo.

74   appropinquant virgines   et adorant tute
        deum venerabili   cinctum iuventute
        gloriantur numinis   in tanta virtute
        quas deus considerans   prevenit salute.

75   causam vie postulat;   aperitur causa
        et laudatur utraque   tantum pondus ausa.
        ad utramque loquitur: "modo parum pausa,
        donec res iudicio   reseretur clausa!"

76   deus erat; virgines   norunt deum esse:
        retractari singula   non fuit necesse.
        equos suos deserunt   et quiescunt fesse.
        Amor suis imperat,   iudicent expresse.

77   Amor habet iudices,   Amor habet iura:
        sunt Amoris iudices   Usus et Natura;
        istis tota data est   curie censura,
        quoniam preterita   sciunt et futura.

78	eunt et iustitie	ventilant vigorem,
	ventilatum retrahunt	curie rigorem:
	secundum scientiam	et secundum morem
	ad amorem clericum	dicunt aptiorem.

79	comprobavit curia	dictionem iuris
	et teneri voluit	etiam futuris.
	parum ergo precavent	rebus nocituris,
	que sequuntur militem	et fatentur pluris.

1 ecce torpet probitas
  virtus sepelitur;
 fit iam parca largitas
  parcitas largitur;
 verum dicit falsitas,
  veritas mentitur.

Refl. omnes iura ledunt,
  et ad res illicitas
  licite recedunt.

2 regnat avaritia,
  regnant et avari,
 mente quivis anxia
  nititur ditari,
 cum sit summa gloria
  censu gloriari.

Refl. omnes iura ledunt
  et ad prava quelibet
  impie recedunt.

3 multum habet oneris
  do das dedi dare,
 verbum hoc pre ceteris
  norunt ignorare
 divites, quos poteris
  mari comparare.

Refl. omnes iura ledunt
  et in rerum numeris
  numeros excedunt.

4 cunctis est equaliter
  insita cupido;
 perit fides turpiter;
  nullus fidus fido,
 nec Iunoni Iupiter,
  nec Enee Dido.

Refl. omnes iura ledunt,
  et ad mala devia
  licite recedunt.

5 si recte discernere
  velis, non est vita,
 quod sic vivit temere
  gens hec imperita;
 non est enim vivere,
  si quis vivit ita.

Refl. omnes iura ledunt,
  et fidem in opere
  quolibet excedunt.

XXV <u>Propter Sion non tacebo</u> (41)

1 Propter Sion non tacebo
   sed ruinas Rome flebo,
     quousque iustitia
   rursus nobis oriatur,
   et ut lampas accendatur
     iustus in ecclesia.

2 sedet vilis et in luto
   princeps, facta sub tributo
     quod solebam dicere,
   Romam esse derelictam,
   desolatam et afflictam,
     expertus sum opere.

3 vidi, vidi caput mundi
   instar maris et profundi
     vorax guttur Siculi;
   ibi mundi bithalassus,
   ibi sorbet aurum Crassus
     et argentum seculi.

4 ibi latrat Scylla rapax
   et Charybdis auri capax
     potius quam navium;
   ibi cursus galearum
   et conflictus piratarum
     id est cardinalium.

5 Syrtes insunt huic profundo
   et Sirenes, toti mundo
     minantes naufragium;
   os humanum foris patet,
   in occulto cordis latet
     deforme demonium.

6 habes iuxta rationem
   bithalassum per Franconem;
     quod ne credas frivolum:
   ibi duplex mare fervet,
   a quo non est qui reservet
     sibi valens obolum.

7 ibi fluctus colliduntur,
   ibi panni submerguntur,
     byssus, ostrum purpure;
   ibi mundus deglutitur,
   immo totus sepelitur
     in Franconis gutture.

8 Franco nulli miseretur
   nullum sexum reveretur
     nulli parcit sanguini;
   omnes illi dona ferunt,
   illuc enim ascenderunt
     tribus, tribus domini.

9 canes Scylle possunt dici
   veritatis inimici,
     advocati curie,
   qui latrando falsa fingunt
   mergunt simul et confringunt
     carinam pecunie.

10 iste probat se legistam,
   ille vero decretistam
     inducens Gelasium
   ad probandum questionem;
   hic intendit actionem
     regundorum finium.

11 nunc rem sermo prosequatur:
hic Charybdis debacchatur,
    id est cancellaria;
ubi nemo gratus gratis
neque datur absque datis
    Gratiani gratia.

12 plumbum, quod hic informatur
super aurum dominatur
    et massam argenteam;
equitatis phantasia
sedet teste Zacharia
    super bullam plumbeam.

13 qui sunt Syrtes vel Sirenes?
qui sermone blando lenes
    attrahunt byzantium;
spem pretendunt lenitatis
sed procella parcitatis
    supinant marsupium.

14 dulci cantu blandiuntur
ut Sirenes, et loquuntur
    primo quedam dulcia:
"Frare, ben je te cognosco,
certe nichil a te posco
    nam tu es de Francia.

15 terra vestra bene cepit
et benigne nos excepit
    in portu concilii;
nostri estis, nostri! cuius?
sacrosancte sedis huius
    speciales filii.

16 nos peccata relaxamus
et laxatos collocamus
    sedibus ethereis.
nos habemus Petri leges
ad ligandos omnes reges
    in manicis ferreis."

17 ita dicunt cardinales
ita solent di carnales
    in primis allicere.
sic instillant fel draconis,
et in fine lectionis
    cogunt bursam vomere.

18 cardinales ut predixi
novo iure Crucifixi
    vendunt patrimonium;
Petrus foris, intus Nero
intus lupi, foris vero
    sicut agni ovium.

19 tales regunt Petri navem,
tales habent eius clavem
    ligandi potentiam;
hi nos docent, sed indocti,
hi nos docent, et nox nocti
    indicat scientiam.

20 in galea sedet una
mundi lues inportuna
    camelos deglutiens.
involuta canopeo
cuncta vorat sicut leo
    rapiens et rugiens.

21   hic piratis principatur
     Spurius qui nuncupatur,
       sedens in insidiis,
     ventre grosso, lata cute,
     grande monstrum nec virtute
       redemptum a vitiis.

22   maris huius non est dea
     Thetis, mater Achillea,
       de qua sepe legimus,
     immo mater sterlingorum,
     sancta soror loculorum,
       quam nos Bursam dicimus.

23   hec dum pregnat, ductor ratis
     epulatur cum piratis
       et amicos reperit;
     nam si Bursa detumescit,
     surgunt venti, mare crescit
       et carina deperit.

24   tunc occurrunt cautes rati
     donec omnes sint privati
       tam nummis quam vestibus.
     tunc securus fit viator,
     quia nudus, et cantator
       it coram latronibus.

25   qui sunt cautes? ianitores
     per quos, licet seviores
       tigribus et beluis,
     intrat saccus ere plenus,
     pauper autem et egenus
       tollitur a ianuis.

26   quod si verum placet scribi,
     duo tantum portus ibi,
       due tantum insule,
     ad quas licet applicari
     et iacturam reparari
       contracte navicule.

27   Petrus enim Papiensis,
     qui electus est Meldensis
       portus recte dicitur;
     nam cum mare fluctus tollit,
     ipse solus mare mollit,
       et ad ipsum fugitur.

28   est et ibi maior portus,
     fetus ager, florens ortus,
       pietatis balsamum:
     Alexander ille meus,
     meus, inquam, cui det Deus
       paradisi thalamum.

29   ille fovet litteratos,
     cunctos malis incurvatos,
       si posset, erigeret;
     verus esset cultor dei
     nisi latus Elisei
       Giezi corrumperet.

30   sed ne rursus in hoc mari
     me contingat naufragari,
       dictis finem faciam,
     quia, dum securus eo,
     ne submergar, ori meo
       posui custodiam.

1   Versa est in luctum
      cithara Waltheri,
    non quia se ductum
      extra gregem cleri,
    vel eiectum doleat
    vel abiecti lugeat
      vilitatem morbi,
    sed quia considerat
    quod finis accelerat
      improvisus orbi.

Refl.   libet intueri
      iudices ecclesie
      quorum status hodie
      peior est quam heri.

2   umbra cum videmus
      valles opperiri
    proximo debemus
      noctem experiri;
    sed cum montes videris
    et colles cum ceteris
      rebus obscurari,
    nec fallis nec falleris
    si mundo tunc asseris
      noctem dominari.

Refl.

3   per convalles nota
      laicos exleges
    notos turpi nota
      principes et reges,
    quos pari iudicio
    luxus et ambitio
      quasi nox obscurat,
    quos celestis ultio
    bisacuto gladio
      perdere maturat.

Refl.

4   restat, ut per montes
      figurate notes
    scripturarum fontes;
      Christi sacerdotes
    colles dicti mystice,
    eo quod in vertice
      Sion constituti,
    mundo sunt pro speculo
    si legis oraculo
      vellent non abuti.

Refl.

5   iubent nostri colles
        dari cunctis fenum,
    et preferri molles
        sanctitati senum;
    fit hereditarium
    Dei sanctuarium,
        et ad Christi dotes
    preponuntur hodie
    expertes scientie
        presulum nepotes.

Refl.   si rem bene notes,
            succedunt in vitium
            et in beneficium
        terreni nepotes.

6   veniat in brevi,
        Iesu, bone Deus,
    finis huius evi
        annus iubileus!
    moriar ne videam
    Antichristi frameam,
        cuius precessores
    iam non sani dogmatis
    stant in Monte Chrismatis
        censuum censores!

Refl.

1 Licet eger cum egrotis,
et ignotus cum ignotis
fungar tamen vice cotis
ius usurpans sacerdotis.
   flete, Sion filie!
   presides ecclesie
   imitantur hodie
      Christum a remotis.

2 si privata degens vita
vel sacerdos vel levita
sibi dari vult petita,
hac incedit via trita:
   previa fit pactio
   Simonis auspicio
   cui succedit datio:
      sic fit Giezita.

3 iacet ordo clericalis
in respectu laicalis,
sponsa Christi fit mercalis,
generosa generalis;
   veneunt altaria,
   venit eucharistia,
   cum sit nugatoria
      gratia venalis.

4 donum dei non donatur
nisi gratis conferatur;
quod qui vendit vel mercatur
lepra Syri vulneratur.
   quem sic ambit ambitus,
   idolorum servitus,
   templo sancti spiritus
      non compaginatur.

5 si quis tenet hunc tenorem,
frustra dicit se pastorem;
nec se regit ut rectorem,
renum mersus in ardorem.
   hec est enim alia
   sanguisuge filia
   quam venalis curia
      duxit in uxorem.

6 in diebus iuventutis
timent annos senectutis,
ne fortuna destitutis
desit eis splendor cutis.
   et dum querunt medium,
   vergunt in contrarium;
   fallit enim vitium
      specie virtutis.

7 ut iam loquar inamenum;
sanctum chrisma datur venum.
iuvenantur corda senum,
nec refrenant motus renum.
   senes et decrepiti,
   quasi modo geniti,
   nectaris illiciti
      hauriunt venenum.

8 ergo nemo vivit purus,
castitatis perit murus,
commendatur Epicurus,
nec spectatur moriturus.
   grata sunt convivia;
   auro vel pecunia
   cuncta facit pervia
      pontifex futurus.

XXVIII <u>Fas et Nefas</u> (19)

1   Fas et Nefas ambulant
    pene passu pari;
    prodigus non redimit
    vitium avari;
    virtus temperantia
    quadam singulari
    debet medium
    ad utrumque vitium
    caute contemplari.

2   si legisse memoras
    ethicam Catonis,
    in qua scriptum legitur
    "ambula cum bonis",
    cum ad dandi gloriam
    animum disponis,
    supra cetera
    primum hoc considera,
    quis sit dignus donis.

3   vultu licet hilari,
    verbo licet blando,
    sis equalis omnibus,
    unum tamen mando:
    si vis recte gloriam
    promereri dando,
    primum videas
    granum inter paleas
    cui des et quando.

4   dare non ut convenit
    non est a virtute,
    bonum est secundum quid,
    sed non absolute;
    digne dare poteris
    et mereri tute
    famam muneris,
    si me prius noveris
    intus et in cute.

5   si prudenter triticum
    paleis emundas,
    famam emis munere;
    sed caveto, dum das,
    largitatis oleum
    male non effundas.
    in te glorior:
    cum sim Codro Codrior
    omnibus habundas.

1   Fortune plango vulnera
    stillantibus ocellis,
quod sua michi munera
    subtrahit rebellis.
verum est, quod legitur
    fronte capillata,
sed plerumque sequitur
    Occasio calvata.

2   in Fortune solio
    sederàm elatus,
prosperitatis vario
    flore coronatus;
quicquid enim florui
    felix et beatus,
nunc a summo corrui
    gloria privatus.

3   Fortune rota volvitur:
    descendo minoratus;
alter in altum tollitur;
    nimis exaltatus
rex sedet in vertice -
    caveat ruinam!
nam sub axe legimus
    Hecubam reginam.

Iste mundus furibundus falsa prestat gaudia,
quia fluunt et decurrunt ceü campi lilia.
laus mundana, vita vana, vera tollit premia,
nam impellit et submergit animas in tartara.
lex carnalis et mortalis valde transitoria
fugit, transit, velut umbra, que non est corporea.
quod videmus vel tenemus in presenti patria,
dimittemus et perdemus quasi quercus folia.
fugiamus, contemnamus, huius vite dulcia,
ne perdamus in futuro pretiosa munera!
conteramus, confringamus carnis desideria,
ut cum iustis et electis in celesti gloria
gratulari mereamur per eterna secula! Amen.

COMMENTARY

1 Cum 'in orbem universum'

(Parts or variant versions of this song are found in seven other mss besides B; see Hilka-Schumann-Bischoff I 3, 72f.)

The 11th and 12th Centuries were a fruitful period for the foundation of new religious orders. So, for example, the Canons Regular, originating in the 11th Century under the reforming pope Gregory VII, became the Augustinian Canons in the 12th. The Cistercian Order, founded at Cîteaux in 1098, laid down a stricter form of Benedictine monasticism. (See R.W. Southern, Western Society and the Church in the Middle Ages (London 1970), Ch. 6.)

This poem amusingly celebrates the Ordo Vagantum, the imaginary order of the Wandering Scholars, and the nature of its Rule. Ever since the 5th and 6th Centuries, the notion of peregrinatio pro Christo and the foundation of numerous monastic establishments throughout Europe had encouraged the movement of restless monks and clerics from one centre to another. Already in the 6th Century it is clear from Benedict's Rule how the hospitality of the monasteries was abused by unspiritual monks. Later, the foundation of universities in Italy, France and Spain accentuated this passion for travel.

This Order of the Wandering Scholars is frequently mentioned in the satirical poetry of the 13th Century. Depicted as the foundation of a legendary Golias,[1] to whom are ascribed epic achievements at table and in bed, it is often described in terms of a religious institute, with headquarters in France, visitations to other communities, and a constitution (described in this poem). All this is comic exaggeration, but the Councils at Trèves (1227), Rouen (1231), Sens (1232/1239) ('ribaudi maxime qui dicuntur de familia Goliae') and Salzburg (1291) criticise and discipline the Vagantes as a sect.[2]

The poem amusingly instructs on membership (stanzas 1-7), food (stanza 8), daily routine (stanzas 9-11), clothing (stanzas 12-13), hospitality (stanzas 14-15).

1   'in orbem universum' A parody of Mark 16.15: 'euntes in mundum universum praedicate evangelium omni creaturae' (sung as the Responsorium on the Wednesday after Pentecost), this is so to say the scriptural justification for the Order.

     sacerdotes . . . cenobite . . . levite sacerdotes here indicates secular priests, living in the world and taking no religious vows:

cenobite ('sharing a common life') are religious in community:

levite are deacons, the order below that of priest. The words sacerdos and levita are familiar to medieval readers from the bible, where levita means a temple-assistant; cenobita was familiar from the writings of Jerome and other Latin fathers who describe monastic life.

ab evangelio 'after reading the Gospel'.

sectam The word used by various councils in condemnation of the Vagantes; see the introductory comment.

salus . . . vite In the familiar double sense of 'salvation of eternal life' and 'safety in this life'.

2   'Omnia probate!' Cf. 1 Thess. 5.21: 'omnia autem probate, quod bonum est tenete' ('scrutinise all things and lay hold of what is good').

vitam nostram, etc. Amusingly turning the accusations of their accusers, for pravi clerici is a term of reprobation more regularly attached to the Vagantes.

in caritate 'out of Christian love'.

3   Marchiones The margrave was originally the governor of territories on the frontier of empire called marcae or marches.

Bawari, Saxones, Australes Suggesting that this poem may have a German provenance. 'All you noblemen of Bavaria, Saxony, Austria . . .'.

decretales 'regulations', strictly the epistulae decretales or rescripts of a pope to a bishop or other ecclesiastical superior on some aspect of canon law.

quod ML = ut.

non liberales 'skinflints'.

4   nos Emphatically placed.

devoti The ironical adjective, again suggesting the reversal of traditional roles.

5   cum rasa corona This is the regular phrase for the tonsure (cf. Anni parte florida, XXIII 38).

cum sua matrona In the Western church, beginning with the papal decretals of Damasus and Siricius in the 4th C., the ideal of celibacy was legalised as the norm for priests and deacons. But the regulation was frequently violated. Councils and popes constantly condemn such marriages; for example, the First and Second Lateran Councils (1123 and 1139) declared them invalid, and popes such as Nicholas II (1059) and Gregory VII (1074) forbade married priests to perform the liturgy. There is a powerful poem in the C.B. (91) which condemns uxorious clerics for presuming to offer mass. Clearly here the Ordo Vagorum proclaims itself more permissive towards married clergy than, e.g. Cardinal Gualo at Paris in 1208, whose Constitutions excommunicates priests and clerics who continue to keep women after admonition. See in general H. Leclercq, D.A.C.L. 2.2. 280ff.

magistrum cum pueris There would presumably be a halo of notoriety around a schoolmaster on the road with pupils.

virum cum persona 'a person of standing'; for this sense of persona, cf. Matt. 22.16, 'non enim respicis personam hominum.'

6   secta 1 n.

This stanza contains only two lines in B (which has 'senio combustos') and no other ms contains it.

7   stature genitive.

in personis 5 n.

8   generis There is a pun here on the two meanings of genus, gender and kind. Since people 'of different kinds' make up the sect, masculine and feminine and neuter pronouns should precede the word secta. (Such play on grammatical paradigms is very common in medieval lyrics; see in general Lehmann 75ff., 152ff..)

qui tot hospitatur 'are offered hospitality in great numbers'.

9   assatura 'roast meat', a biblical word; cf. 2 Kings 6.19: 'David partitus est universae multitudini assaturam bubulae carnis unam'.

hordei Stricter monastic orders like the Carthusians had a meatless diet, often subsisting on coarser grain like barley-meal. William of Malmesbury remarks that the Cistercians serve meat only to the sick.

faciat 'would do'.

10   matutinas The rule of St. Benedict enjoins that Matins be sung at the eighth hour of the night, about 2 a.m. The poet now explains why the Goliards will have no such disturbance of their slumbers.

plane 'utterly'.

phantasmata The word is both classical and biblical. Perhaps the hymn of Compline, Te lucis ante terminum ('procul recedant somnia / et noctium phastasmata') was in the author's mind.

11   popinas is Patzig's emendation of pruinas.

Hashardi The personification of chance; OF hasard, derived from the Arabic iasara (L. Laistner).

12   uti dupla veste   In the Order's regulations for dress, only one thickness of garment is permitted. This stanza is concerned with the upper part of the body; either tunica or pallium is worn.

tunicam qui recipit   'sich vorbehält' (Laistner), 'keeps in reserve', a common classical sense of the word.

reiicit   'casts off', the regular classical meaning (Livy 23.8, 'togam ab umero'; Cic., Pis. 55), here in the sense of losing.

Decius, the god of gaming, is the personification of decius (OF dez), dice. Cf. C.B. 195.2a: 'qui perdit pallium / scit esse Decium / fortunae nuntium / sibi non prospere!.

conteste = teste, a medieval usage.

cingulum   The word loses its predominant sense of 'lady's belt' and becomes more general in sense in the medieval period.

13   in imis teneatur   'must hold good for the lower also'.

camisia . . . bracis   The camisia is properly a nightshirt (Isid., Orig. 19.22.29) stretching below the knee. Trousers, the mark of the barbarian to the Romans, were a common Gallic garment.

caliga . . . calceus   caliga is a leather boot, calceus a shoe with a top as distinct from solea, a sandal; 'if boots are among his possessions, he must not carry shoes'.

14   The obligation accepted by monastic houses to help strangers was so frequently exploited by unscrupulous travellers that on occasion they were coldly received; see Helen Waddell's amusing account in The Wandering Scholars, Ch. 8. At the headquarters of the Ordo Vagorum, the poor traveller will be able to try his luck at the gaming-table!

15   vultum condolentis   The poverty registers 'suffering on its owner's face'.

16   Probably in parody of Walter of Châtillon, Mor.-sat.Ged. 13.1: 'singulorum singulos mores explicare / reprobare reprobos et probos probare / et hedos ab ovibus veni segregare'. (Cf. Matt. 25.32).

Notes

1   Ermini has shown how the Fathers, notably Augustine and Bede, regarded Goliath as a special antagonist of Christ. It is probably from this that the Golias legend developed.

2   For the background see H. Waddell, The Wandering Scholars, Ch. 8: de Ghellinck, 505f.
On this poem see R. Schieffer, Mitteil. Inst. österreich. Geschichtsforsch. 82, 1974, 412ff.

II Estuans intrinsecus

(The poem appears in about 30 mss besides B, five of them in London, and two each in Cambridge and Oxford.)

On the author, the Archpoet, see the Introduction, p. 2. Stanzas 8-9 suggest that the poem was written at Pavia. Rainald, the poet's patron, and Otto the Count Palatine were in Pavia in March-June 1162, and again in autumn 1163, in the course of journeying as ambassadors to the Pope. The poem is to be attributed to that period; it became known as 'The Confession' in the 13th Century.

The poem shows a characteristic convergence of classical and Christian themes. On the one hand, it is clear that the confession of Ovid, Amores 2.4 is the model;[1] on the other hand the poem is a confession in the technical Christian sense, with the pattern of confession, contrition, purpose of amendment, imposition of penance, and absolution.[2]

Stanzas 14-19 also appear at Archpoet 4.10-15, and Langosch[3] has persuasively argued that they spoil the structure of the poem here. He would therefore argue for their exclusion, and set up the poem as follows:

1-3	Dissatisfaction with the poet's own inconstancy
4-9	Confession of sexual faults
10	Confession of gambling
11-13	Confession of drink
20-25	Repentance and request for pardon.

The pattern of 3/6/1/3/6 which this exclusion of 14-19 effects is certainly striking.

The patterning of scriptural and classical evocations is particularly noteworthy. Initially the Archpoet expresses self-disgust in a string of scriptural reminiscences in which he sustains the roles of a Job, of the author of Wisdom, of the worldly man condemned by Paul. In his confession of sexual foibles, Ovidian echoes are prominent, and when he turns to gambling, Horatian passages are brought to mind. After the confession of sins comes the promise of self-amendment, and here the Archpoet reverts to scriptural evocation to express his conviction that he is reborn.

1   The coincidence of biblical reminiscences should be noted in this stanza.
intrinsecus Recalls Gen. 6.6: 'tactus dolore cordis intrinsecus . . . '.
in amaritudine etc. The Archpoet here depicts himself as a second Job. Cf. Job 10.1: 'loquar in amaritudine animae meae . . . '.
folio sum similis So Job 13.25: 'folio, quod vento rapitur.'

2   The poet passes from the Old to the New Testament.

   <u>Viro sapienti</u>, etc. Cf. <u>Matt</u>. 7.24: 'viro sapienti, qui aedificabit domum suam super petram.'

   <u>fluvio labenti . . . nunquam permanenti</u> Perhaps a reminiscence of both <u>Job</u> 14.2: 'nunquam in eodem statu permanet', and of Hor., <u>Ep</u>. 1.2.42f.

3   <u>feror . . . veluti . . . navis</u> Cf. Ovid, <u>Am</u>. 2.4.8: 'auferor ut rapida concita puppis aqua'; but also <u>Wisdom</u> 5.10: 'transierunt omnis illa . . . tamquam navis quae pertransit fluctuantem aquam'.

   <u>ut . . . vaga fertur avis</u> Cf. <u>Wisdom</u> 5.10: 'aut tamquam avis, quae transvolat in aëre.'

   <u>quero mei similes</u> For the proverbial expression 'birds of a feather' ('similis similem sibi quaerit'), see the refs. in Manitius, <u>Die Gedichte des AP</u> (1929).

4   <u>gravis</u> 'oppressive'.

   <u>dulciorque favis</u> Cf. <u>Ps</u>. 18.11: 'dulciora super mel et favum'.

5   <u>via lata</u>   Cf. <u>Matt</u>. 7.13:   'lata porta et spatiosa via est quae ducit ad perditionem'.

   <u>implico me vitiis</u> Cf. 2 <u>Tim</u>. 2.4: 'nemo militans deo implicat se negotiis saecularibus.'

   <u>voluptatis avidus</u> Cf. 2 <u>Tim</u>. 3.4: 'voluptatum amatores magis quam dei.'

6   <u>presul</u> This is Rainald Dassel, the Archpoet's patron and Archbishop of Cologne.

   <u>discretissime</u>   i.e. <u>iudicandi peritus</u> and therefore here = <u>iustissime</u>.   Cf. Archpoet 4.1: 'vir discrete mentis.'

   <u>corde mechor</u> Cf. <u>Matt</u>. 5.28: 'qui viderit mulierem ad concupiscendum eam, iam moechatus est eam in corde suo,'

7   <u>legem sequi duram</u> The 'hard law' of chastity was still harder in the <u>respublica clericorum</u>, and the poetry of the clerks is often focussed on the celibacy issue. Cf. C.B. 121a: 'non est crimen amor quia si scelus esset amare / nollet amore Deus etiam divina ligare'.

   <u>levium corporum</u> i.e. lēvium; for such lēvitas of the body, cf. Macr., <u>Sat</u>. 7.7.8.

8   <u>Papiae</u> i.e. Pavia, renowned as a centre of luxurious life. Cf. the comment of Landulf of Milan, that as Rome is known for its buildings and Ravenna for its churches, so Pavia is known for its luxurious life.

   <u>digito . . . venatur</u> The gesture with the middle finger, called the <u>impudicus</u>, is well known in classical poetry; cf. Juv. 10.53, 'medium ostendere unguem', and

Martial 6.70.5f. 'impudicum ostendis digitum mihi'. Cf. Volo virum vivere (XIX, 4).

predatur 'captures'.

9   Hippolytum Cf. Ovid, Am. 2.4.32, 'illic Hippolytum pone, Priapus erit'.

in tot turribus Pavia, like S. Gimignano, was famous for its turreted appearance in the 12th Century.

turris Alethie This is the reading which has the support of the mss, and those who defend it gloss the word alethia with virtus, truth in the sense of integrity or castitas; Peter Damian (d. 1072) speaks of turris castitatis: Haureau's conjecture Aricie (the town in Latium called after Hippolytus' wife, and symbolic of Chastity, (cf. Raby, Speculum (1932) 394) is attractive, but the penultimate i is short, as Raby says (see his note in S.L.P. 2, 184). Unger proposed Acrisie, 'the Acrisian maiden' who is Danaë, the daughter of Acrisium, who enclosed her in a tower (Ovid, Met. 4.610, Claudian, In Eutr. 82f. etc). But in addition to the similar metrical objection, this tower was breached; cf. Walter Map, De nugis curialium 4.3: 'Gold broke through the barriers of the town of Acrisius, and melted the viriginity of Danaë, guarded by many a rampart.'

10   redarguor It is of course dangerous to regard the poem as closely factual, but here and in 20 the suggestion is made that the Archpoet was being accused by others in Rainald's retinue.

ludus . . . nudo Cf. Hor., Ep. 1.18.21: 'quem damnosa Venus, quem praeceps alea nudat'.

cudo Again Horatian; A.P. 440f., and for the sentiment. Ep. 2.2.51f.

11   Requiem eternam The first words of the Introit or Entrance hymn in the Mass for the Dead: 'requiem aeternam dona eis Domine . . .'.

12   mori Compare Ovid's statement at Am. 2.10.35 of his intention to die in lovemaking.

potatori In parody, of course, of Luke 18.13, 'deus propitius esto mihi peccatori.'

13   imbutum nectare An Augustan phrase - cf. Ovid, Met. 4.252, 'imbutum caelesti nectare corpus', and Hor., C. 1.13.16, 'quinta parte sui nectaris imbui.'

14   Those who defend the retention of the next six stanzas against Langosch's charge that they destroy the harmony of the structure contend that the content is relevant, because it portrays the poet as a man who thrives on wine and good company, unlike other poets. But I am not convinced.

loca vitant publica For poets who shun public life, cf. Hor, Ep. 2.2.65,77: A.P. 298, etc.

parum ML = paulum.

15   poetarum chori Cf. scriptorum chorus at Hor., Ep. 2.2.77.

possint The subjunctive is consecutive (for quod = ut, I 3n.).

16   unicuique, etc. Cf. 1 Cor. 7.7.: 'unusquisque proprium donum habet ex Deo'.

17   The repetition of the first line effectively aids the contrast between the Archpoet thirsty and the Archpoet in his cups.

purius 'of the finer sort'.

vinum tale For the sentiment, cf. Hor., Ep. 1.5.9: 'fecundi calices, quem non fecere disertum?'.

18   Nasonem Note that Ovid is in a sense the model of the poem. See the introductory comment before this poem.

19   spiritus poetrie So Apoc. 19.10, spiritus prophetiae; poetria means poetess in the classical period but poetry in ML.

in arce cerebri The image of the head as citadel forms a part of that famous account of the human body in Plato's Timaeus which is cited by 'Longinus'. It appears in Latin in Seneca's Oedipus 185 (arx corporis), Claudian IV, Cons. Hon. 235: Sid. Apoll. 5.238.

20   mee proditor pravitatis The sentiment provides another connexion with Ovid; cf. Am. 2.8.26: 'et veniam culpae proditor ipse meae.'

seculo frui 'to enjoy the pleasures of the world'; saeculum in this sense is biblical and ecclesiastical.

21   iam nunc Biblical; Gen. 42.15: 'iam nunc experimentum vestri capiam', Exod. 33.5, etc.

secundum . . . regulam Cf. 2 Cor. 10.15, etc.

mittat in me lapidem Cf. John 8.7: 'qui sine peccato est vestrum, primus in illam lapidem mittat.'

parcat vati Horatian; cf. Ep. 1.7.11: 'parce tuo vati.'

22   virus evomui The phrase is at Cic., De Amicitia 87.

homo videt faciem, etc. Cf. 1 Kings 16.7: 'homo enim videt ea quae parent, dominus autem intuetur cor.'

Iovi It is one of the conventions of the poets of this period, who are so conscious of classical models as well as Christian literature, that they describe the Christian God by the name of Jupiter. This should not be regarded as a deChristianising motif: see the comments of Watenphul-Krefeld, p. 35.

23   spiritu renascor Cf. John 3.5: 'nisi quis renatus fuerit ex aqua et spiritu sancto, non potest inire in regnum dei.'

quasi modo genitus Cf. the Introit for Low Sunday: 'quasi modo geniti infantes . . . ' recalling 1 Pet. 2.2: 'sicut modo geniti infantes, rationabile sine dolo lac concupiscite.'

vanitatis vas Cf. Acts 9.15: 'vas electionis.'

amplius = diutius.

24   electe i.e. chosen as bishop; cf. 6 above.

penitenciam 'a penance'. At Confession, once the penitent has confessed his sins (1-13), he expresses a firm purpose of amendment (22-23), begs God's pardon, and is required to perform some penitential act imposed by the priest. Nowadays this is usually a spiritual exercise, but in the medieval period penitents were frequently required to atone for their sins publicly, or to do some good works.

25   parcit, etc. Cf. Ps-Ovid, De mirabilibus mundi 106f.:

'parcere prostratis scit nobilis ira leonis,

tu quoque fac simile quisquis dominaris in urbe.'

Notes

1   Cf. H. Unger, De Ovidiana in Carminibus buranis quae dicuntur imitatione (Strasburg 1914); see the nn. at 3, 9.

2   See the analysis in the Watenphul/Krefeld edition of the Archpoet.

3   Deutsches Archiv (1942) 400ff.

III <u>In taberna</u>

(The song is found in full only in B, but fragments of it and variations on it are found in other mss; see Hilka-Schumann-Bischoff, No. 196.)

      The drinking song here as often parodies the liturgy of the Church (see stanzas 3-4), the company drinking to the various categories for which they pray on more solemn occasions.

1   <u>humus</u> 'the earth, our resting-place'. Cf. 2.7 below.

      <u>ludum</u> i.e. game of chance.

      <u>insudamus</u> The Archpoet after gambling loses his shirt but sweats mentally; cf. II, 10: 'frigidus exterius / mentis estu sudo'. For <u>insudare</u> cf. Hor., <u>Sat.</u> 1.4.72.

      <u>nummus est pincerna</u> Money is the steward because possession of it dictates whether you get wine or not. <u>pincerna</u> is a word originally Greek but common in late and medieval Latin.

      <u>queratur</u> ML = <u>quaeratur</u>.

2   <u>indiscrete</u> 'without discernment', i.e. 'in rude fashion'. Cf. <u>discretus</u> in <u>Estuans intrinsecus</u> (II 6).

      <u>saccis induuntur</u> Having lost their clothes by gambling, they necessarily wear the garb that others voluntarily wear as penitents. Cf. <u>2 Kings</u> 3.31, <u>Jonas</u> 3.5, etc.

      <u>pro Baccho</u> i.e. the stakes are cups of wine.

3/4   Some scholars draw attention to the parallels here with the Good Friday liturgy, in which the second part of the action ('oratio fidelium') was a series of public prayers for the Church, the Pope (cf. 4.7), for 'bishop, priests, deacons, sub-deacons, acolytes, exorcists, readers, doorkeepers, confessors, virgins, widows and all God's holy people' (cf. 3.5, 3.7), for 'political rulers' (cf. 4.7), etc.

      But more important are the correspondences with the <u>Missae Votivae</u> and the <u>Orationes Diversae</u> appended to them in the <u>Missale Romanum</u>. These include masses 'Pro peregrinantibus et iter agentibus' (cf. 4.6) and 'In commemoratione omnium fidelium defunctorum' (cf. 3.6), and prayers 'Pro constituto in carcere vel in captivitate' (cf. 3.3), 'Pro salute vivorum' (cf. 3.4), 'Pro navigantibus' (cf. 4.3), 'Pro inimicis' (cf. 4.4), and 'Pro publice poenitentibus' (cf. 4.5).

3   <u>primo</u> sc. <u>bibunt</u>.

nummata The adjective nummatus is Ciceronian, but this noun is a medieval usage, with the sense of 'pennyworth'.

libertini 'the emancipated'.

semel . . ter 'They drink once for the imprisoned, three times for the living . .'.

sororibus vanis 'worldly nuns', or perhaps nuns are 'fruitless' in the eyes of these 'libertini'.

silvanis 'Knights of the woods' in their role as huntsmen.

4 perversis A 'pervert' friar is one who secedes from religious belief and practice, the antonym of 'convert'.

dispersis The monk's life was essentially claustralis, of the cloister, so here again the drinkers drink to renegade religious.

sine lege 'indiscriminately'.

5/6 The repetitions here remind us of a later composition, the Sequence for Corpus Christi, entitled Lauda Sion, composed by St. Thomas in 1264:

> 'sit laus plena, sit sonora
>
> sit jucunda, sit decora,
>
> mentis jubilatio . . .
>
> sumit unus, sumunt mille,
>
> quantum isti, tantum ille,
>
> nec sumptus consumitur.
>
> sumunt boni, sumunt mali
>
> sorte tamen inequali
>
> vite, sed interitus . . . '

It may well be that this is a characteristic form of rhythmical song, and P. Lehmann, Die Parodie 184f. shows a further example (see 5 below).

5 miles . . . clerus For this regular antithesis between knight and cleric, see XXIII.

ille . . . illa In a 16th-C. Venetian ms (cf. Novati, Carmina Medii Aevi, Florence 1883, 66ff.), we read:

> 'iam lucis orto sidere
>
> statim oportet bibere . . .
>
> bibat ille, bibat illa,
>
> bibat servus et ancilla . . .'

rudis The contrast with magus suggests that the meaning is 'ignorant'.

6 presul et decanus The contrast between puer and canus in the previous line is now reversed, bishop and deacon representing high and low in the ecclesiastical hierarchy. praesul is a classical word, meaning 'leading dancer'; hence in late Latin it means a director, and is taken over in Christian Latin to mean bishop.

73

7   <u>nummate</u> 'pence'; cf. 3.

ubi ipsi Peiper suggests <u>ubi sic</u>.

<u>sine meta</u> = <u>sine fine</u>, not a classical usage.

<u>sic nos rodunt</u> 'because of this, the whole world slates us'; <u>rodunt</u> in this sense is classical, especially common in satire.

<u>omnes gentes</u> Cf. <u>Ps</u>. 46.2: 'omnes gentes, plaudite manibus'.

<u>et cum iustis</u> Cf. <u>Ps</u>. 68.29: 'deleantur de libro viventium, et cum iustis non scribantur.'

IV Exul ego clericus . . .

(The poem is found only in B.)

    The poet describes the familiar situation of the poverty-stricken wandering cleric, who has journeyed to France for higher studies, and is begging for money and clothing from a local dignitary.

1   Exul 'away from home'.

    tribulor Ecclesiastical (Tertullian, Ambrose, etc.).

    multotiens 'again and again' (post-classical).

2   insudare Horatian (cf. Sat. 1.4.72).

3   calore relictus 'abandoned by all warmth'.

4   laudibus Lauds are the morning prayer of the divine office, so called because of the recurrence of laudate in the Psalms sung (Ps. 148-50). Lauds and Vespers are the most important hours of the Day Office, which is why they are mentioned especially.

    misse (sc. possum interesse). This term for the eucharistic liturgy (a late form of missio or 'dismissal') goes back at least to the 4th C., when Ambrose, Ep. 20, uses the phrase missam facere for 'to celebrate mass'.

    vespere Vespers were sung in the late afternoon before dark.

    dum cantetur finis Vespers culminated in the communal singing of the Magnificat.

5   decus . . . insigne 'Your excellency, N., since you are so illustrious'. The use of the second person plural in addressing a higher personage is already common in the 12th C. The omission of the name perhaps allows the poem to be used on different occasions. dum is ML = cum ('since').

    suffragia The word is common in the sense of financial help: cf. Du Cange, s.v.

6   Martini In reference to the famous incident when St. Martin of Tours gave a beggar half his cloak at Amiens (Sulpicius Severus, Vita Martini, 3), a gesture followed by the vision of Christ which impelled him to enter the religious life.

7   polorum The word is frequent in the sense of 'heaven' from the 4th C.

    conferat The ms has conferunt, but the rhyme with transferat and the general sense make the change certain.

V Omittamus studia

(This song appears only in B)

Though this poem, with its conventional theme of 'Gather Ye Rosebuds', may appear a spontaneous composition, the pervasive evocations of Horace and of Juvenal should be noted. The poet deploys these to present a wholly classical-pagan view of life and love, extending even to the concept of deity (stanza 3), and excluding that biblical element which so often equips the poet with a double vision and a fruitful tension of ideologies.

1   Omittamus studia Cf. Hor., C. 4.12.25: 'verum pone . . studium lucri . . .'

dulce est desipere Ibid 28: 'dulce est desipere in loco'.

tenere Genitive; 'innocent'.

seriis intendere Cf. Hor., Sat. 1.1.27: 'amoto quaeramus seria ludo'.

res est, etc. This is Herkenrath's suggestion for filling the hiatus in the ms. Laistner proposes: 'insudandoque virtuti / vitia rependere.'

(Refl.) lascivire suggerit 'prompts us to frolic'.

2   ver etatis For the metaphorical sense, cf. Catullus 68.16: 'iucundum cum aetas florida ver ageret'; Ovid, Met. 10.85 (a more probably inspiration): 'aetatis breve ver'. Cf. also Omnia sol temperat (XVI, 2).

damnum patitur 'suffers harm'. Cf. Juv. 10.209f.: 'aspice partis / nunc damnum alterius . . .'.

sanguis aret Cf. Juv. 10.217: 'minimus gelido iam in corpore sanguis . . .'

morborum familia Cf. Juv. 10.218: 'circumsilit agmine facto / morborum omne genus'.

3   imitemur superos Cf. X below: 'Amor habet superos / Iovem amat Iuno . . .'.

et amores teneros 'an innocent love-affair'. For the plural, cf. Virg., Aen. 4.292, Ovid, Met. 9.519, etc.

venentur Laistner's reading is preferable to venantur of the ms because the entire stanza is hortatory.

retia 'hunting-nets'; the poet will have Ovid, A.A. 1.45 in mind, 'scit bene venator cervis ubi retia tendat'.

numinum It is tempting to read iuvenum; see the quotation in the next note.

choreas virginum Cf. Hor., C 1.9.15f.: 'nec dulces amores / sperne, puer, neque tu choreas / donec virenti canities abest / morosa . . .'.

4   que fit facilis 'easily obtained', going with copia.

<u>asto</u> Cf. <u>C.B.</u> 76.6

<u>me michi surripiunt</u> 'steal my heart away'. Cf. Hor., <u>C</u>. 4.13.20: 'quae me
surpuerat mihi; <u>C.B.</u> 104, 'michi me surripuit'.

VI Deus pater, adiuva

(The poem is found in one other ms; cf. Hilka-Schumann-Bischoff, 1.3, 207).

In this witty poem there is a dialogue between two brothers. The first lies ill in some danger (stanzas 2, 6) from which he proposes to extricate himself by entering a monastery. The second advances various arguments against this plan - his own solitude (stanza 3), the possibility that the hazard is not mortal (stanza 5), the rigours of monastic life (stanzas 7, 9), the grief of parents (stanza 11), the parting from a young cleric, perhaps a pupil and the apple of his eye (stanza 13). The native hue of resolution is gradually sicklied over with the pale cast of thought, and the decision is finally postponed.

1   crastinum Supply diem.

2   vult The subject is provided by mors in 1, or by the person who is the source of danger.

3   The second brother speaks.
    secus 'consult your welfare another way'.

4   orphanus Not 'an orphan' (cf. 11), but 'brotherless'.

6   angustia . . . 'the distress afflicting my heart'. The singular is frequent in the Vulgate; cf. Gen. 42. 21 angustiam animae.
    quod est ML = ut sit.

7   tibi The mss have mihi; Patzig's emendation is necessary.
    ieunant William of Malmesbury remarks that the Cistercians take only one meal a day between September and Easter; and the meteoric growth of this Order in the 12th C. (cf. Southern, W.S.C.M.A., ch. 6) as against the more moderate Benedictine regimen would make such rigours appear the norm.

9   donat The subject is regula from 7; Hilka-Schumann-Bischoff tentatively suggests donant here.
    fabas ac legumina See above, I 8.
    potum aque Again referring to the stricter orders; the Benedictines permitted wine.

10 Dionysia In CL the festival of Bacchus, frequently mentioned by the comic poets; here the sense is 'wine-revels'.
    et de dapibus 'after feasting', is Patzig's suggestion for the mss reading ubi et dapibus. Heraeus suggests leta dapibus.

11 vel 'Or (if the austerity argument fails) . . .'.

plangit The subject is gemitus. Schmeller needlessly proposed plangunt.

12   The reply is a twofold evocation of scripture, the first couplet recalling the
      Christian ideal of peregrinatio pro Christo (cf. Gen. 12.1, etc.), the second the
      day of judgment (Apoc. 20. 11ff., etc.).

13   ars dialectica Dialectic or logic formed with grammar and rhetoric the
      trivium, the first three of the liberal arts. It claimed a controlling discipline
      over the other six, laying down the bases of all utterance. Martianus Capella
      4.336 makes Dialectic say: 'meique prorsum iuris esse quicquid Artes ceterae
      proloquuntur.'. In the poem here the lament is against that capacity for logical
      argument which is able to counter all objections to retirement to the
      monastery.
      esses cognita 'would you had never been discovered.'

14   videris Peiper's emendation of videbis, which the rhythm will not allow. This
      stanza has only two further lines in the mss, 'diligis illum parvum / clericum N.
      pulcherrimum.' The text as printed is the suggestion of Peiper, where N. stands
      for a name with triple syllable like Gualterum.

15   Hilka-Schumann-Bischoff has a full stop after nescio and not after exilio but my
      punctuation seems preferable.
      hëu Scanned monosyllabically in CL, but again as two syllables in Dulce solum
      (VII). It is not found with the dative in CL, but cf. Virg., Aen. 10.849: 'heu nunc
      misero mihi demum / exsilium infelix', perhaps in the poet's mind here.

16   fletibus Gröber's necessary emendation of floribus.

VII Dulce solum

(There are five other mss besides B containing the song (see Hilka-Schumann-Bischoff I 1, 197).

In B and L, the order of stanzas 3 and 4 is reversed. But the order as printed seems to me preferable, with the nature of the love (igne novo) described before the reflexion on its sorrows. B alone has a further stanza, but its generalised tone is out of tune with the personal note of stanzas 1-4:-

> 4a   Heu dolor, quam dira premia!
>
>   flamma calent amantes nimia;
>
>   nova nutrit Venus suspiria;
>
>   urgent eam quandoque dulcia
>
>   nimis!

The mss B and C have an extra word appended to stanzas 1-3 (1 exul: 2 igne: 3 gravis), and B has similarly the word usque appended to 4. These are to be envisaged as later additions to the original. Apart from the fact that they detract from the rhyming effect, the feebleness of usque in 4 (and its appearance only in B), the superfluousness of gravis to the proverb in 3, the duplication of igne at 2 end and 3 beginning, all argue against these words having been part of the original poem.)

The poem has been variously described as 'a song of departure before travelling for study' (Laistner) and a poem on 'the madness of love' (Brinkmann). There is an element of both. Formally, the poem is in the tradition of the syntaktion, the speech of departure in which the poet praises the country left behind. But the main theme is the sorrows of love. The two motifs are joined together by the fact that the love-experience is depicted as the cause of departure; and if the poet is adopting the persona of a cleric, the journey is explicable as the necessary way of avoiding a crisis in his calling. This is a dimension of the 'sorrows of love' theme which should not be disregarded - the plight of the 12th century cleric divided between inclination and vocation.

1   domus ioci, thalamus gratie 'merry house and pleasant lodging'.

2   consortem is the reading of CL; B alone has expertem, which is much more likely to be an 'improvement' on consortem than vice versa.

     vobis 'so far as you are concerned'.

3   vera proverbia 'the truth of the proverb'.

     ubi amor ibi miseria Similar sentiments are found at Plaut., Pers. 179.

4   quot sunt apes So the mss CS; the reading of BL is flores. But Ovid is clearly
the inspiration of this stanza, and he writes (A.A., 2.517ff.): 'quot lepores in
Atho, quot apes pascuntur in Hybla / caerula quot bacas Palladis arbor habet
/litore quot conchae, tot sunt in amore dolores.' The Sicilian mountain Hybla
was of course renowned for both bees and flowers (Virg., Ecl. 1.55, 7.37, etc.).
Dodona frondibus The ancient oracle of Zeus at Dodona was situated in an oak
grove.
quot natant pisces Cf. Ovid, Pont. 2.7.28: 'quot natant pisces aequore . . . '.

VIII Letabundus rediit

(The poem is only in B.)

This poem is a lyrical description of the joys of returning spring. Frequently in the C.B. this theme is followed by the poet's declaration of his own feelings of love associated with the rebirth of nature. But here the references to love are more generalised, and the poem's central concern is the aptness of the season for the joys of love.

1   avium concentus 'the symphony of the birds' is a Ciceronian phrase; cf. Cic., Leg. 1.21.

ver iocundum So also at Cat. 68.16.

serenatur 'becomes bright'; the verb is often transitive in classical poetry.

redolens temperiem 'diffusing pleasant warmth'.

Flora Here the goddess of flowers, whose festival on April 28 (Ovid, Fasti, 5.195ff.) marked the coming of spring and ripening love. Hence the exploitation of the name elsewhere in the C.B. for a girl ripe for love; cf. XXIII below.

2   risu Iovis 'by heaven's smile'.

Note the antithesis of lines 2 and 4.

⟨cuius omnis regio⟩ The solitary ms has qui sublato bravio, a line obviously inserted in error from 5, for it is meaningless here. Some such line as ⟨cuius omnis regio⟩ is required (Hilka-Schumann-Bischoff, ad loc.).

ad instar 'like'; the phrase becomes frequent in late and medieval Latin. We have here the comparison direct between the heat of the season and the heat of passion.

3   estivantur Only the active form occurs in CL; 'enjoy the summer season'.

Dryades . . . Satyrorum The names establish not only the poet's learning but also the non-Christian ethos of the poem. Nymphs and satyrs are of course regularly associated in classical poetry (Hor., C. 1.1.31, 2.19.4. etc.); cf. XXIII 9 below.

Tempe Often in CL in the sense of the picturesque valley in general (Hor., C. 3.1.24, Virg., Georg. 2.469, etc.); the form is neuter plural as regularly.

his . . . concinit 'sings in harmony with them'.

philomena On the form, see XIV, 4. The nightingale is a commonplace also in vernacular lyrics of the period, e.g. Jaufré Rudel, 1.1ff.

4   purpurata This form is in classical poetry used only of exalted persons, and purpureus is used of flowers, but purpuratus is more conveniently accommodated to rhythmical rhyming here.

miti . . . susurrio susurrium is a post-classical form. Virgil uses levis susurrus of the bee (Ecl. 1.56).

gryllus The word is classical, but the classical poets prefer cicada, a symbol of summer at Ovid, A.A. 1.271.

iubilo 'glad cry'; cf. Calpurnius, Ecl. 1.80.

5   Veneris . . . ara Cf. the n. in 3 above. on Dryades . . . Satyrorum.

bravio bravium is a late form of brabeum (βραβεῖον), a word used in the Vulgate for 'prize' (1 Cor. 9.24).

sine spe For the technical sense, see X 7.

IX Tempus adest floridum

(This poem is found only in B; in P, a collection of songs published in 1582 and re-edited in 1910 by G.R. Woodward, Piae cantiones ecclesiasticae et scholasticae veterum episcoporum, the first stanza of the poem is followed by three further stanzas which convert the ode into a hymn to the Creator. See Hilka-Schumann-Bischoff, ad loc.)

After the conventional nature-introduction (stanza 1), the poem depicts a group of maidens deciding to sport in the fields. But the third stanza develops the treatment into a much more personal love-appeal from one of the suitors.

1   vernales [mox] in omnibus   Hilka-Schumann-Bischoff punctuates with a semicolon after vernales, takinq the adjective with the preceding flores; but such a variation between sentence-ending and line-ending would be unusual, and I prefer to take vernales with mores: 'in spring all things change their ways'. Hilka-Schumann-Bischoff also retains mox in the text with a query in the app. crit.; I excise it for reasons of rhythm.

2   ludamus 'let us sport amongst them'.

cum clericis On the cleric as flirtatious suitor, see above all Anni parte florida (XXIII below); 82 and 172 are others in the C.B. with this motif.

3   This abrupt change of tone and viewpoint from maidens to male suitor leads some commentators to doubt whether this stanza belongs to this poem, or alternatively to speculate on the loss of an intermediate stanza.

Helena . . . Paris See XXIII 12 n. below.

talis The rhyme is unsatisfactory; W. Meyer ingeniously suggested par his.

X Amor habet

(The poem exists in one ms besides B,F (Florence Laur. Edili 197, 13th Century.)

The theme is the universal sway of Cupid - on Olympus, on the sea, in the underworld; and the two forms of that love, which Andreas Capellanus labels amor purus and amor mixtus. The poet expresses his loathing of amor mixtus, the love which includes sexual intercourse, for this is turpis voluptas (stanza 3). His love is the amor purus which falls short of consummation (stanza 8), and which is described by Andreas, 1.6 H: 'purus amor . . . procedit ad oris osculum lacertique amplexum et verecundum amantis nudae contactum, extremo praetermisso solacio'. This theme of the two forms of love can be traced back through the treatises of the Arabs in Spain (notably the treatise of Avicenna on love, translated by E. Fackenheim in Medieval Studies (1945)) to the dialogues of Plato, notably the Phaedrus.

1   Amor 'Love possesses the gods above'.

(Refl.) virgino The word appears as a deponent in Tertullian: 'play the virgin with', 'flirt innocently with'.

aro non in semine The biblical image (cf. Eccli. 6.19 'qui arat et seminat') is used to describe amor purus.

pecco sine crimine pecco is here used of venial sinning which does not include fornication; for crimen in this latter sense, cf. Ovid, Met. 9.24.

2   amor Love constrains both flexible innocence and unbending roughness.

flexu 'yoke'.

rhinoceros It was a popular belief that a unicorn (not differentiated from a rhinoceros in the middle ages; cf. T.H. White, The Book of Beasts (N.Y. 1954) 20f. quoting a 12th C. ms as saying that the unicorn is called also rhinoceros by the Greeks) could be captured through the charms of a pretty girl, with whom the animal would sport and so allow her to entice it into captivity. The tradition goes back to a famous Alexandrian work on the behaviour of animals, the Physiologus (2nd C. AD or earlier):-

    1000:   ἐκεῖνος ἄλλεται ἐξ αὐτῆς, τὸν κόλπον τῆς καθίζει
                 καὶ τοὺς μάστους τῆς τέρπεται, θηλάζει τοὺς ὡς βρέφος,

This work was translated into Latin, the oldest mss dating to the 8th C. (F. McCulloch, Medieval Latin and French Bestiaries (Chapel Hill, 1962). Isidore, Etym. 12.2.13 reflects acquaintance with it: 'tantae autem esse fortitudinis ut nulla venantium virtute capiatur; sed, sicut asserunt qui naturas animalium scripserunt, virgo puella praeponitur quae venienti sinum aperit, in quo ille omni ferocitate deposita caput ponit, sicque soporatus velut inermis capitur'. The unicorn consequently has a history as a symbol of chastity which goes back to Cyprian; cf. Anal. Hymn. 20.276 and 188. C.B. 93a also mentions the motif; the suggestion that it refers to Abelard because he includes it in his Historia Calamitatum is fanciful. Harl. 4751 (White, 20f.) says: 'Our Lord Jesus Christ is a unicorn spiritually, about whom it was said 'And he was beloved like the son of unicorns'. It is accordingly possible that the poet may intend a reference to those in the celibate calling generally.

3   corruptas   See the preliminary note on amor mixtus. The indiscriminate association of harlots and matrons makes the allusion clear.

4   calesco Ovidian (Met. 3.272, Her. 18.177, etc.).

5   ludus For the technical sense, see 8.

puelle 'The sport my girl affords'.

precordia . . . felle Physiologically the praecordia is the breast and the fel the gall-bladder (Celsus 4.1: 'iecur a dextra parte sub praecordiis; ex inferiore parte ei fel inhaeret'). In the case of Cecilia, 'there is no bile in her heart'.

6   Cecilia In C.B. 88a, the ms T has nata est Cecilia, where other mss have virgo nostra nascitur.

7   flos Symbolises virginity not only in Christian writing but also in classical poetry; cf. Cat. 62.46.

non est, etc. With the implication of the child that may follow from amor mixtus.

spes has a technical sense in courtly love, as Andreas Capellanus explains. When the girl encourages a suitor to pay court to her, she 'spem largitur'. He then has to prove himself by his exertions. There are several poems in the C.B. which are devoted to the theme of spes. 163, Longa spes et dubia, reflects the mental morbidity induced by a long period of waiting; 164, Ob amoris pressuram and 171, 'De pollicito / mea mens elata / in proposito vivit, animata /spei merito: tamen dubito / ne spes alterata cedat subito . . . ' are other examples.

8   comtemplari, etc. These are the quinque lineae amoris, briefly alluded to at Ovid, Met. 10.342, and spelt out in detail by Donatus on Terence, Eun. 638: 'quinque lineae amoris, scilicet visus, allocutio, tactus, osculum sive suavium, coitus'. Cf. also Porphyrio on Hor., C. 1.13.16. It is something of a commonplace as a topic in the 12th C.; see for example C.B. 72 and 154. It is

perhaps of significance that we find an adapted version of it in the first dialogue of Andreas Capellanus.

9   decet . . ludum . . tenere   These words all stress the innocent nature of this relationship of amor purus.

XI Transit nix et glacies

(This poem appears only in B.)

In this lyric, the motif of quickening nature provides the barest of introductions; the main theme of the love-hatred induced by an indifferent lady begins in the very first stanza. The highly literary texture of the poem should give us pause before we label it a delineation of spontaneous emotion.

1   Transit nix . . . Favonio Evoking above all else Hor., C. 1.4: 'Solvitur acris hiems grata vice veris et Favoni'.

materies The 'matter' of the earth is the sprouting of flowers: the corresponding 'matter' of the poet is his sprouting love. But materies also bears the sense of 'subject', and both meanings are intended here.

(Refl.) temporis Centrally placed to be taken with both gaudia and lascivia.

2   agnosco vestigia . . . flamme veteris After the Horatian evocation in 1, the poet here turns to Virg., Aen. 4.24: 'agnosco veteris vestigia flammae'.

nove . . . Veneris Like Dido, the poet describes a new love.

a quo For suggested emendations of the corruption, see Hilka-Schumann-Bischoff. I suggest a, que manent, 'O, what sorrows await lovers more than all others!'.

3   gravior mens 'my mind, more burdened than before . . . '.

plus asperior The pleonasm accentuates the arrogance of the proud lady.

4   amor . . . odium Recalling Ovid, Am. 3.11.3f. 'pectusque leve in contraria tendunt, / hac amor hac odium', rather than Cat. 85, since Catullus was virtually unknown.

furatur Cf. Omittamus studia (V 4) 'me michi subripiunt'.

5   cantu Presumably an ablative of separation, not found with finio in CL.

superis Reinforcing the classical flavour of the poem.

unde = a qua.

XII Tempus accedit floridum

(The poem appears only in B.)

This poem presents perhaps the commonest of the themes of love in these lyrics, the aspiration not yet attained, in the pattern which is the most conventional. The burgeoning of nature, descriptive of the work of Venus in the natural order, is the opening motif. This is followed by the wretchedness of the poet who loves a maiden as yet unpricked by Cupid's arrow, so that the poet feels out of joint with the whole of nature.

1   temere 'readily' or 'willingly', in CL found regularly in the negative expression non temere.

2   ludere 'frolic'. The word is almost technical in these lyrics for the flirtation which is innocent and falls short of total love. Cf. Amor habet superos (X 8, above). The poet is troubled with dreams which go beyond mere flirtation. gratiam 'favour'.

3   solacio In the technical sense of the consolation afforded by the loved one.

4   The last two lines are rightly obelised by Hilka-Schumann-Bischoff because they are technically defective. Note the poor rhyme in contrast to the final lines of the earlier stanzas; and nam pro te gemitus is two syllables short. It looks as if these last two lines have been provided by a later contributor whose virtuosity in technique does not match his nice sense of an appropriate ending.

XIII <u>Dum Diane</u>

(The poem is found only in B. There are in the ms four further stanzas (see Hilka-Schumann-Bischoff, I.2.20f.) which Dronke (<u>M.L.R.E.L.L.</u>, 306ff.) considers integral to the poem. I remain unconvinced by his two arguments - first, that the technical exposition of stanza 6 (which he interestingly compares with Hildegarde's <u>Causae et curae</u>) is central to the poem, and secondly that the well-known parody <u>Dum domus lapidea</u> (<u>C.B.</u> 197; see Lehmann, I 195) has echoes of stanzas 6 and 8. On these alleged echoes, 'ex alvo leta fumus'/'ex domo strepunt gressu', and 'caret anchora'/'carens cena', one can only remark that the connections are tenuous in a parody sustained much more closely in stanzas 1-4. So far as the relevance of stanzas 5-8 to stanzas 1-4 is concerned, stanzas 5-6 and 7-8 are wholly different from each other in tone, though they are variations on the same theme of sleep and love. Stanzas 5-6 are a disquisition so technical, and their theme is so detached from that of stanzas 1-4 (sleep after love-making and love-making after sleep are extraneous to stanzas 1-4) that these stanzas cannot belong. Stanzas 7-8 are no more than a series of commonplaces on the theme of love and sleep, almost every phrase of which is found in other lyrics. The banal tone distinguishes them not only from stanzas 1-4 but also from 5-6. This impression of three separate compositions is confirmed by plagiarisms; stanza 5.5-6 is borrowed from stanza 3.1-2, and in turn stanza 7.12-14 from 5.1-2. In short stanzas 5-6 and 7-8 are separate pieces of <u>Zudichtung</u>.)

    The theme of the poem proper (stanzas 1-4) is the blessings of night for the weary lover, the soothing effects of the wind and dew reinforced by the healing effects of sleep. Love-making is irrelevant. So too is man-made music to which Dronke gives mistaken prominence. <u>vi chordarum</u> in stanza 1 is the music of the Zephyr. In stanza 3 the poet describes the images induced in the mind by sleep, so 'Orpheus' must be emended to 'Morpheus', the vision-purveyor mentioned by Walter Map, <u>De nugis curialium</u> 4.6 and a god familiar to literate men through Ovid, <u>Met.</u> 11.634, 647.

1   <u>vitrea</u> 'glistening'; the word is used of dew by Ovid, <u>Am.</u> 1.6.55.

    <u>lampas . . . rosea luce</u> Lucretius 5.610 writes 'rosea sol alte lampade lucens', and though the <u>De rerum natura</u> is little-known in the 12th C., this looks like a deliberate reminiscence. <u>lampas</u> is used of the moon by Valerius Flaccus 7.366 and Nemesianus, <u>Cyn.</u> 1.30.

    <u>dulcis aura</u> The phrase is found with different sense at Virg., <u>Georg.</u> 4.417.

    <u>etheri</u> Ablative (of separation); the -<u>i</u> form, common in ML, is required for the rhyme.

vi chordarum vi and not vis is the reading of the ms, and should be retained; note that in the parody Dum domus lapidea the corresponding line reads: vi bursarum pectora. Just as the West wind removes clouds from the sky so he removes love-burdens from the heart 'by the power of his strings'.

2   iubar ('radiance'), an appropriate word because of the evening star's brightness; Ovid, Fasti 2.149 similarly uses it of the morning star.

3   quot Manitius' emendation from quod.
     surrepit Ovidian; Fasti 3.19: 'blanda quies furtim surrepit ocellis'.
     poris This Greek word for a passage is earlier found in Ambrose and Isidore.
     ipsum = antidotum. It is this line which has inspired the additional 5-6 and 7-8, but the poet's point is precisely the blessing of sleep for one in the sorrows of love, which makes both the disquisition in 5-6 and the uninhibited activity described in 7 inappropriate.

4   Morpheus For the reading, see the preliminary comment on this poem.
     impellentem Governing segetes, 'a gentle wind inclining the ripe harvest'.
     per harenas puras 'along glistening courses of sand'.
     molendin<ari>orum Apart from the improvement of the rhythm, this reading gives added point to the final line. The beasts of the mill 'who in sleep steal the light of our eyes' were usually blind or blindfolded. The scriptural exemplar was of course Samson, who at Judges 16.21 was blinded and made to grind the corn, and the passage was allegorised by Christian commentators like Paulinus of Nola, Ep. 23.12: 'The enemy will gouge out our eyes, imprison us, and allot us to the asses' task of turning the millstone'. Cf. Lucius-turned-ass in Apuleius, Met. 9.11.3, grinding the corn velata facie, luminibus obtectis.
     The main point of this memorable stanza, however, is that sleep brings relief by robbing the poet of his waking sight and by soothing his mind with the gentle rustle of wind on corn, the murmur of streams, and the sound of the turning of the mill.

XIV O comes amoris, dolor

(The poem is found only in B and in the Fragmenta Burana; see Hilka-Schumann-Bischoff 1.3, 8*.)

The regular pattern in the 12th-Century love-lyric is to begin with an idyllic description of nature at the change of season, and to pass from the quickening in nature to the quickening of human love. In this poem there is a subtle reversal of the scheme, with the description of nature in the final stanza; and this because nature and its glories are here a consolation for the lover in the toils of unrequited love. The theme of dolor in love is of course perennial, and in these lyrics it is a frequent motif; see Dronke, Index s.v. sorrows.

1   cuius . . . solor 'for whose ills I find poor consolation'.

     an habes . . . 'Is there any remedy for you?'

     quem i.e. me.

     dirum . . . exilium Suggesting that the lady is high-born, and that it would be dangerous to declare his love.

     pro qua, etc. 'Paris would not have preferred Helen's company to hers'. The Helen-Paris liaison is a frequent theme in the learned lyric; cf. C.B. 99, 101-3.

2   cuius nomen The reverential address perhaps suggests the background of court or castle for this love-liaison, real or imagined. Cf. C.B. 166.3: 'me sciat ipsa magnanimum / maiorem meo corpore / qui ramum scandens altissimum /fructum queram in arbore . . .'. See further Dronke, 305.

     quod Consecutive, as aften in ML.

     nec = ne . . . quidem.

     mei mali 'for what reason accountable to me in my sorrow . . .'; mei mali is a genitive of exclamation.

     neminem? I punctuate with an interrogation here.

3   amo . . . hamo Cf. Andreas Capellanus 1.3: 'amor is derived from amo, meaning to catch or be caught, for the lover . . . wishes to catch another on his hook (hamo)'. Cf. Isidore, Etym. 10.1.5 for the fanciful derivation.

     nec vicem reciprocat 'But she does not reciprocate my feelings'.

     ut paradisum To the literate Latinist the word connotes the double sense of 'park' and the Eden in which the Creator has set this beautiful second Eve.

4   philomena This medieval variant of philomela is common in 12th-Century poetry: cf. Walter of Châtillon, S. Omer 351, 23.1, 'ferit vocis iaculo

/Philomena sidera'; (cf. VIII 3, XXII 3), etc. The popularity of the nightingale-motif may be in part attributable to the ?12th Century <u>Carmen de philomela</u> which was attributed to Ovid in the 12th century; for a revised text, see P. Klopsch, 'Carmen de philomela', in <u>Europäischen Mittelalter; Festschrift für Karl Langosch zum 70. Geburtstag</u> (Darmstadt 1973) 173ff.

XV Huc usque, me miseram

(The poem appears only in B, where a further stanza and a refrain appear at the beginning:-

1a	Tempus instat floridum,	Refl.	Eya
	cantus crescit avium,		qualia
	tellus dat solacium		sunt amoris gaudia

but these lines are obviously to be expunged as an irrelevant accretion. In the rhyme-scheme, the first four stanzas form a unity by the rhyming of the final lines, and likewise the second four; subsequently the final rhymes are a/b/a/b/a. Allen suggested a stanza-rearrangement of 9, 11, 12, 10, but both the sense and the rhyme-scheme are defensible as the stanzas already stand. In the final stanza, Peiper supplies <iam>; some such addition before or after sum is clearly required.)

The pregnancy theme presents yet another variation of the love-lyrics, and the girl as spokeswoman is also unusual. The poignant tone may beguile us into underestimating the art of the poet, revealed both by subtlety of rhymes and by clarity of structure. After the first stanza as introduction, the girl traces the causes of her misery in an outward pattern. She begins with herself and her discomfort (stanza 2), passes next to her parents (stanza 3), then from family to burghers (stanzas 4-9), and finally from her German (?) city abroad to France and her lover's exile (stanzas 10-13).

1   rem Deliberately ambiguous, denoting the 'affair' specified in line 3, but then elaborated in 2 (res mea) to indicate the pregnancy.

2   gravide The adverb is not used in CL.

3   improperat Primarily biblical; Matt. 27.44, etc.

4   inpalam The word palam is found in the Vulgate as an indeclinable noun. So Luke 8.17: . . . 'quod non cognoscatur et in palam veniat'. The form inpalam is subsequently found in Christian writers.

    ludere Usually in these lyrics in the sense of love-flirtation, but here more generally 'frolic'.

6   pulsat 'elbows'; cf. 7.

    transierim 'until I have passed by'. The perfect subjunctive after dum, unusual even in ML, is required for the rhyme-scheme.

9   quid percurram singula? As Raby remarks, there is an Ovidian flavour about this interrogatio, reinforcing the impression of the craftsman at work.

10   ex eo 'Because of this notoriety'.

12   in Franciam   Indicating a German (or less probably British or Italian)
      provenance for the poem.
      a finibus ultimis 'in the furthest reaches'; cf. in CL a cornu dextro, etc.

13   <iam> See the preliminary textual comment.

(The poem is found only in B.)

Again here there is the customary overture - the description of nature in spring introducing the theme of love. Of similar poems in Provencal, Lazar comments: "C'est l'ouverture presque classique des poèmes d'amour". But unlike Tempus accedit floridum (XII), the theme here is of a love secure through the fides of the absent lover and his confidence in the fides of his lady.

1   subtilis is used of fire by Lucr. 6.225; the sense is that the sun in April lacks the density of heat of the dog-days, and hence is 'fine'.

animus herilis The adjective is with reference to Venus, since the allusion to Cupid follows: 'our mistress' purpose hastens toward love'.

iocundis Dative, 'to the happy heart'. The concept of joy as a true quality of the courtly lover is emphasised also in the poetry of the troubadours. Cf. gaudere in 2.

2   in sollemni vere 'at spring's ritual coming'.

in tuo vere 'In the spring of your own youth'. Cf. Omittamus studia (V.2) and the references there. tuo is emphatic, relating the burgeoning of the girl to that of nature.

probitas Like fides, probitas is a courtly quality constantly emphasised in the treatise of Andreas Capellanus. It is the honesty of manners which makes a partner totally reliable.

tuum retinere 'the loyalty and honesty to keep faith with your lover'.

3   sum presentialiter absens in remota 'Though absent afar (understand parte or regione after remota) I am with you wholly in heart and wholly in mind'. presentialiter (not found before the 8th C.) limits absens.

volvitur in rota The wheel of love is visualised as the wheel of Ixion (Ovid, Met. 4.461ff. 'volvitur Ixion', etc.) on which the lover is turned and broken. Cf. Plaut., Cist. 206ff.: 'iactor, crucior, agitor / stimulor, vorsor / in amoris rota'.

XVII Iove cum Mercurio

(This poem appears in B and in P. P has only the four stanzas printed; B has two others between 2 and 3, as follows:-

    2a si valeret Zëuxis   istam contemplari,
       pictura Tyndaridem volens imitari,
       statim quinque cederent huic exemplari.

    2b si futuram cerneret   Mulciber amicam,
       non dotata Phronesi scanderet lecticam,
       sed illam querens coniugem relinqueret antiquam.

P is the older and better ms. But apart from this consideration, these two stanzas are irrelevant to the theme of the poem. They introduce the motifs of painting (Zeuxis modelled his Helen on five beauties of Croton; cf. Pliny, N.H. 35.64 and Abelard, P.L. 178, 257), and of literature (Martianus Capella's Marriage of Philology and Mercury, esp. 2.143). But notice that it is Mercury, not Vulcan as here, who is the bridegroom of Philologia 'dowered by Phronesis' (line 2) her mother. These themes are irrelevant to the sustained connexion made between the course of the stars and the course of true love. Hence their excision.)

The poet here wittily harnesses the contemporary interest in astrology to furnish an exordium for his love-lyric different from the usual description of the seasons. It is important to realise how largely astrology figures in the schools as the underside of scientific and philosophical studies, being often exploited to attack Christian tenets. "Astrologers were not 'false magicians', but people who measured nature; for them the real practitioners of 'false magic' were people who busied themselves with religion, any kind of religion." (F. Heer, The Medieval World, ch. 12). As natural scientists preaching the doctrine of determinism, many of these astrologers condemned the notions of prophecy and miraculous events implicit in Christian teaching, and Christian thinkers were frequently involved in the rebuttal of such attacks or in the investigation of their claims about physical 'laws'.

Since the names of the planets and the signs of the zodiac were common knowledge in the schools, they could be exploited to make the witticisms noted in stanza 1 below. But the main point of the poem is epitomised in the final word. The love of the poet and his lady is as predetermined as the movements of the heavenly bodies.

1   Iove cum Mercurio, etc. Ever since antiquity professional astrologers had
      calculated the position of dominant constellations at the time of an individual's

97

birth to prophesy his fortunes. The poet's lady was born 'when Jupiter and Mercury were in Gemini'. Jupiter is a favourable star, and its being in Gemini suggests a favourable omen for the lovers. 'Venus was driving Mars out of Libra' indicates that harmonious love will be theirs. <u>virgo nascitur</u> has a play on the rising of the constellation Virgo. 'When Taurus lay hidden' presages a love without animal brutality.

On the astronomical lore of the stanza, I have consulted Professor H.A. Brück, the Astronomer Royal for Scotland. He writes "The stanza does indeed make sense astronomically. The first and third lines indicate that the girl must have been born on some evening of March or April. Taurus having set and Mercury being in Gemini (the constellation of the Zodiac which lies immediately to the east of Taurus) must mean that Mercury was an evening star. Since Mercury is always close to the sun, it is best seen in the evening at such eastern 'elongations from the sun' as occur in March and April . . . Venus in Libra must have been a morning star, the constellation Libra being about 120 degrees to the east of Gemini."

2   <u>legibus</u> i.e. <u>Naturae</u>.

      <u>ignibus . . . ignis</u> Being born under identical stars (<u>ignibus</u>) has made the fire of their passion to correspond.

3   <u>cui liceat . . .</u> 'who can infiltrate his guile'. The poet thinks of a mischievous whisperer like the one described in XVIII below.

      <u>non in vanum</u>, etc. 'It is not for nothing (<u>in vanum</u> = <u>vane</u> as at Sen., <u>Hippol.</u> 182, etc.) that our stars spangle the sky'.

4   <u>obicit</u> The subject is to be supplied from 3.2.

      <u>sic determinatur</u> See the introductory comment.

XVIII Lingua mendax

(The poem appears only in B.)

This witty poem is devoted to the perennial theme, the allegation that the poet has been unfaithful to his lady, and his protestations of innocence are undercut by the ambivalence reflected in the deities by whom he swears.

It is helpful to recall that prudentia, a sense of discretion, was a central preoccupation in the conduct of courtly loving. The twelve rules for love in Andreas' De Amore include an injunction not to allow others to be privy to your own love-affair, and another is the command never to divulge the liaisons of others. "When love is publicised" states one of the 31 canons in the second book, "it rarely endures". Amongst the 21 judgments on individual love-problems there is the condemnation of a knight for divulging his own love-affairs to others; he is sentenced to deprivation of all prospect of love, and to be the object of contempt of all ladies.

There are several poems in the C.B. reflecting this desire for secrecy. A case in point is Si linguis angelicis (77):-

> pange lingua, igitur, causas et causatum,
> nomen tamen domine serva palliatum,
> ut non sit in populo illud divulgatum
> quod secretum gentibus exstat et celatum . . .

Or again, Rumor letalis (120):-

> cautius ama, ne comperiatur!
> quod agis, age in tenebris,
> procul a fame palpebris.
> letatur amor latebris

Vernacular poets of the period condemn the jealousy of malevolent gossip, as in Bernard Marti's second poem (ed. Hoepffner, Paris 1929). So too Andreas' treatise repeatedly condemns scandal-mongering.

1 . detruncari Usually of decapitation in CL.

3 In the ms, 4 comes before 3, but this would disturb the sequence of adjurations in 4, 5 and 6.

deus . . . dei Note that both Christian God and classical deities are called to witness in this amusing stanza.

reus-rei The words are etymologically connected (Festus: 'reus dictus est a re quam promisit ac debet'), and juxtaposed by Plaut., Trin. 2.1.12; Cic., Verr. 2.2.94, but our poet makes more of the jingle.

4   pro Dane sumpsit auri sc. formam from the next line. For Jupiter's entry as a golden shower into the tower where Danaë was enclosed by her father, see XIX 1 n.

in Europa 'in the case of Europa'; cf. Ovid, Met. 2.836ff., etc. The well-known amatory exploits of Jupiter here, and of the other Olympians in 5, make the protestation ambivalent.

5   Phebum For Apollo in the love-role, cf. Ovid, Met. 1.453ff. (Daphne), 2.542ff. (Coronis).

Martem In his Greek persona as Ares, he is lover of Aphrodite.

qui Note the causal sense of the relative.

Cupido Perhaps following Mars here because in literature and art Cupid/Eros is usually represented as his son.

6   mittis Continuing the apostrophe to Cupid from the previous stanza.

8   tam decenter 'in such splendid proportion', in appreciation of the lady's vital statistics.

9   quoniam . . . Blondes being more at a premium than brunettes.

10   Lines 3, 4 are in reverse order to that in the ms, but the transposition proposed by Bojunga allows indentical patterns in 10.1-3 and again in 10.4-11.2.

11   Parthus sine telis A commonplace, but the poet perhaps recalls especially Ovid, A.A. 1.210: 'telaque, ab adverso quae iacit hostis equo'.

nisi fallar, non falleris A fine ambivalent ending; at one level, 'I won't be false to you if you aren't false to me', but at another, 'You won't be deceived, if I'm not mistaken!'.

XIX Volo virum vivere

(The poem occurs in one other ms besides B.)

This poem initially purports to be a declaration of revolt against the conventions of courtly wooing, but the recusatio in the final stanza shows that the cri de coeur is ironically sustained in the first four stanzas.

The whole sequence of humiliating dependence demanded of a suitor is outlined by Andreas Capellanus in his treatise. When the suitor requests the lady's ear, she may reject him at once or offer him hope (spem largiri). If she offers him hope, he must then prove his worth (probitas) by unceasing labour in her name. She may test him by declaring a moratorium on their relationship, or even by using fallacia, for example by pretending that other suitors are in attendance.

The structure of the poem is clear. Stanza 1 describes the conduct the suitor wishes to impose on himself, and stanza 2 the characteristic conduct of ladies, which he rejects. Stanza 3 reiterates the doctrine of equality, and belabours the notion central to courtly love, that the lady stands at a higher level of excellence. Stanza 4 reverts to his own probitas and the kind of girl it makes him look for. But then the final stanza renounces all the claims to equality so loudly voiced; and this palinode has more point than the amusingly abject surrender. The treatise of Andreas Capellanus (I.6H) reveals that if a lady undertakes the correptio here demanded, she acknowledges that there is a love-relationship. The noblewoman in the dialogue refuses to offer this service because it would compromise her; 'correptionis autem officium non assumam, quia illud amantibus dumtaxat debetur obsequium'. So when the poet says, 'I'm damned if I'll go through the courtly rigmarole, because I want a nice girl on the level - but on second thoughts I'll renounce all this if you'll set me right', he is playing an elaborate ploy to become her amator.

1   virum vivere viriliter The alliteration and repetition conspire to present an inflatedly manly figure soon to be pricked in 5.

fortior quam Iupiter 'a better man than Jupiter'.

procari commercio vulgari A reference to the famous story in Ovid, Met. 4.697ff. in which Jupiter seduced Danaë by appearing in the form of a golden shower (cf. also Servius, ad Aen. 7.372: Hor. C. 3.16.1: Ovid, Am. 2.19.27ff., A.A. 3.631ff.). This becomes in the Middle Ages a parable for the victory of money over virtue; hence this reference by the poet to 'wooing by sordid transaction'.

2   gravi supercilio 'with stern contempt'.

maiorem terminum 'a more distant limit', in reference to the tendency of the courtly lady to defer a decision until the probity of the suitor became certain.

bubus aratrum preficiam In this proverbial equivalent of 'putting the cart before the horse', the boves represent the man the aratrum the woman. Bubus is the more regular classical form of the dative/ablative plural.

plaudens ludere quam plangere delusus The neat verbal play, with chiasmus and alliteration reinforcing the antithesis, should be noted; plaudens here = 'contentedly' and plangere = 'lament', but the primary sense of both verbs is 'to beat'.

3   hanc aleam 'this game of chance', comparing the suitor's wooing to a throw of the dice.

granum . . . paleam For such wheat/chaff contrast, the biblical passage at Matt. 3.12 ('congregabit triticum suum in horreum, paleas autem comburet igni inexstinguibili') is the original inspiration.

pari lege fori 'on the equal terms of the courts'.

ne prosternar 'so I don't have to prostrate myself shamelessly before a woman's virginity'. In setting the lady on a level above the suitor, writers like this poet frequently evoke the thought of the Virgin Mary.

4   pene = paene, though there may a double entendre here.

Hippolyto Also cited as the personification of chastity by the Archpoet in II 9 above.

tam subito que seducat 'so fast as to lead me astray . . .'. The punctuation of Hilka-Schumann-Bischoff, with a full-stop after subito and not after digito, is unacceptable, for this Hippolytus does not allow himself to be seduced 'by eyes and beckoning finger'.

digito Cf. II 8 above.

hec Emphatic.

protervitas Cf. Hor., C. 1.19.7.

5   tue reus dulcedini, etc. 'I'm a prisoner to your charms; I was forgetting how exquisite you are'.

corripe The full sense of the word is 'rebuke and correct'; see the quotation from Andreas in the preliminary comment to this poem.

XX Dum curata vegetarem

(The poem appears only in B.)

This lament for the decline of courtly love is described within the framework of a dream; compare the well-known debate between Wine and Water, Cum tenerent omnia medium tumultum, a long poem in the Goliardic metre, likewise recounted in a dream. A woe-begone Cupid, no longer the dominant power of Ovid's Amores, describes the decline in the behaviour of suitors which has caused his influence to wane. His precepts are no longer being observed, especially the commands to keep love-liaisons secret (stanza 9), to avoid vulgar boasting (stanza 10), to exalt love by virtuous conduct and to keep it unsullied by prostitution or marriage (stanza 11). It is worth comparing the 31 canons for love listed by Andreas Capellanus, which include:-

> Love does not usually survive being noised abroad (13).
> Honesty of character alone makes a man worthy of love (18).
> Marriage does not offer a good excuse for not loving (1).
> One should not seek love with women with whom it is disgraceful to seek marriage (11).

The message is hardly serious. The poet amuses his audience by describing Cupid in the mantle of Job (see stanza 6 n.). It is possible that there is parody of Walter of Châtillon's lament for the good old days also; apart from the echo in stanza 6, Walter's well-known Missus sum in vineam (O.B.M.L.V., no. 198) uses the metrical combination of three Goliardic lines followed by the 'authoritative' hexameter as in stanzas 6-11 here.

1   dum ML = cum.

curata . . . darem The exordium is a learned evocation of Hor., Sat. 2.2.80f.: 'alter, ubi dicto citius curata sorori / membra dedit, vegetus praescripta ad munia surgit'.

animalis . . . naturalis The contrast is between the dominium exercised by the strength of the living being (animalis virtutis, which is suspended in sleep) and that exercised by the power of nature.

2   pharetratus Used of Cupid at Ovid, Am. 2.5.1, Met. 10.525.

crinali torque Hilka-Schumann-Bischoff punctuates crinali, torque, but the sense is improved by taking crinali as adjective and translating 'despoiled of his curly locks', the implication being that he has torn them in grief.

manu . . . tactis 'handled with brute force'.

nunquam talis 'his appearance unprecedented'.

3   membra sc. mea.

membris organicis 'faculties of speech'.

4   cultus Referring to hair and wings.

contrectate 'roughly handled'.

5   singulis sc. interrogationibus.

6   vertitur in luctum Lehmann pointed out the interesting parallel in Walter of Châtillon, who writes in XXV below:-

>versa est in luctum / cithara Waltheri,
>
>non quia se ductum / extra gregem cleri . . .

organum Walter in that poem evokes Job 30.31: 'versa est in luctum cithara mea, et organum meum in vocem flentium'. Our poet makes Cupid a suffering Job.

absinthio 'wormwood', a favourite word of Walter, as in Omer 351, 22.

virtus 'strength', as regularly in the Vulgate.

me vis . . . For this 'authoritative' hexameter, cf. Ovid, Rem. 139: 'otia si tollas, periere Cupidinis arcus'.

7   artes amatorie . . . a Nasone tradite Ovid's A.A. was the bible of courtly love. Chrétien de Troyes tells us (Cliges, ad init.) that he translated it, and Andreas Capellanus regularly quotes it.

modernorum The word develops from modo, and is found as early as Cassiodorus.

turpiter abutitur The line does not scan as a hexameter. Hilka-Schumann-Bischoff considers the possibility of the excision of the whole stanza, which would bring exact balance between the two halves of the poem; Sedgwick suggested abiicitur.

8   voluptativus . . . subductus 'alienated from the base pleasures of the world'; suggesting quite mistakenly that Ovid epitomises that honourable fidelity in love which despises mere sensuality.

qui sibi notus erat 'those acquainted with him'; for the 'authoritative' hexameter, cf. A.A. 2.501.

sapienter 'wise' loving above all connotes the restraint and discretion which ensures secrecy.

9   Veneris mysteris . . . cistis In the ritual of mystery-religions, the vessels and utensils were kept in a sacred box, the cista. Ovid exploits this image to stress the need for secrecy in love, and our learned poet evokes the Ovidian context:

'praecipue Cytherea iubet sua sacra taceri; / admoneo veniat ne quis ad illa loquax. / condita si non sunt Veneris mysteria cistis . . . ' (A.A. 2.607ff).

precipue, etc. The authority is here a direct quotation; see the previous note.

10 sine re iactantiam 'boasting without the actuality'.

eheu, etc. Cf. Ovid, A.A. 2.625: 'at nos nocturnis titulos imponimus actis'. (titulos imponimus = 'we advertise').

11 moribus sc. optimis.

in prostibulo Biblical (Ezech. 16.24, etc.).

redigitur in pactum 'reduced to a contract', a reference to marriage (cf. Juv. 6.25), which some theorists of courtly love regarded as totally alien to true love. Cf. X. 3 above.

XXI Lucis orto sidere

(The poem is found only in B.)

For the genre of the pastourelle, see the Introduction, p.5, where the conventional patterns are outlined. On this base, Lucis orto sidere superimposes a further dimension of sophistication. There is a deliberately sustained biblical and liturgical evocation here which contrives to depict the shepherdess as an earthly Virgin Mary. It was a frequent custom for knights of chivalry to dedicate themselves to the Virgin and to carry her portrait on their armour. In this poem note the several touches, notably in stanzas 3-4, which idealise the shepherdess in this way. It is interesting to note the parallel development of a religious pastoral in French literature, e.g.:

> L'autrier matin el mois de mai
> regis divini munere,
> que par un matin me levai,
> mundum proponens fugere,
> en un plesant pre m'en entrai,
> psalmos intendens psallere,
> la mere Deu ilec trouvai,
> iam lucis orto sidere . . . [1]

What is of the greatest interest in our poem is that the traditional elements of the folk-pastoral are coloured with the association of Christian theology and biblical imagery. Thus the sheep can symbolise Christian man, the wolf the devil, the knight Christ himself and the shepherdess, with her Virgin persona, the Church. The poet may well have in mind the poem of Venantius Fortunatus on the holy cross, Crux benedicta nitet:

> ' . . . traxit ab ore lupi qua sacer agnus oves'.

1 Lucis orto sidere This is the exordium of a number of Christian hymns, and the poet exploits it to strike at the outset the appropriate religious tone. Note especially the traditional hymn for Prime, 'Iam lucis orto sidere / Deum precemur supplices', which would immediately rise to the lips of a 12th-C. litteratus.

   pastorali The word has a double connotation, rural and ecclesiastical.

2 virgo speciosa The adjective familiar from the Song of Songs (2.13: 'surge, amica mea, speciosa mea, et veni') is often applied to the Virgin.

3   salve rege digna This evoked in the contemporary mind the Salve regina, one of
    the oldest Marian antiphons, traditionally ascribed to Hermann the Cripple, and
    a popular hymn in 12th century devotion: see O.D.C.C. ad loc.

4   que non novit hominem The shepherdess replies with words similar to those
    used by the Virgin Mary at the Annunciation: Luke 1.34, 'quoniam virum non
    cognosco'.

6   dum ML = cum

    quod . . . ML = se sic ovem perdere.

    me . . . uxore See the comment in the Introduction on this motif of the genre.

7   ovis . . . redempta Again the language evokes religious overtones, as in Wipo's
    Sequence for Easter: 'Victimae paschali laudes immolent Christiani / Agnus
    redemit oves . . .'.

Notes

1 CF. A. Jeanroy, Les origines de la poésie lyrique en France au Moyen-Age   (Paris
1899), 489.; Raby, S.L.P. II 334.

XXII Estivali sub fervore

(The poem appears only in B.)

This too is a Pastourelle (there are half-a-dozen in all in the C.B.; see P.S. Allen, Medieval Latin Lyrics (Chicago 1931, Ch. 6) but without the added sophistication of religious symbolism such as we found in Lucis orto sidere. In this poem the poet has not sought to give primacy of emphasis to the dialogue. He has sought a balance between the description of the locus amoenus (stanzas 1-3) and the encounter (stanzas 4-6), an example of the rejection-motif in which the shepherdess refuses the gallant's advances. The witty rhymes within each stanza and between the final lines should be noted.

1   Estivali sub fervore 'When summer's heat was commencing'. aestivalis is in Cl. a rare variant of aestivus.

sub olive . . . decore Indicating the southern mise-en-scène.

2   quovis 'of every kind imaginable'.

picturato Used of a flower-bedecked area by Statius, Theb. 6.58.

Plato In Phaedrus 230B, Plato describes just such a scene, with the tree, the spring (πηγὴ χαριεστάτη), the shade, and the pleasant breeze(τὸ εὔπνουν ἀγαπητόν). Cic., De Or. 1.28 has a similar description. But there is no need to posit a direct borrowing, because the locus amoenus is already a stylised feature in ancient literature (cf. Hor., A.P. 17), and in ML poetry the stock motifs are observable in the compositions of Matthew of Vendôme, Alan of Lille, Peter Riga and others. See Curtius, Ch. 10.

3   subest At the bottom of the picture, so to say.

vene Ovidian in this sense of 'course' (Trist. 3.7.16).

philomene See XIV 4 above.

cantilene Nominative. The word is common in both classical prose (Cic., De Or. 1.105, etc.) and the Vulgate (Eccli. 47.19).

paradisus Christian writers naturally exploit the convention of the locus amoenus to visualise Paradise. See Curtius, Ch. 10, n. 31.

4   iocundari Biblical (Apoc. 11.10, etc.) and Christian.

pastorellam This word, which gives its name to the genre, does not appear till the 12th C.

sine pari 'peerless'.

mora The indifference to quantity in the developed rhythmical poetry can be measured by the appearance in the identical position of the stanza of mora (1) and mōra here.

5   Flora Note that the goddess Flora describes her haunts in Ovid, Fasti 5.207ff.

6   sevi Spanke's emendation from Suevi, retained by Hilka-Schumann-Bischoff, is certain. Note the similar final stanza of C.B. 158, after the shepherdess has been seduced:-

> si senserit meus pater,
> vel Martinus maior frater,
> erit michi dies ater;
> vel si sciret mea mater,
> cum sit angue peior quater,
>   virgis sum tributa!

XXIII Anni parte florida

(The poem is found in a dozen mss, including L (Brit. Lib. Harley 978) which contains also C.B. 42 and 191.)

Though the poem's setting evokes the genre of pastoral, and though several motifs and structural features have been rightly regarded as the influence of the epithalamium,[1] Anni parte florida is essentially a literary disputation, a genre which goes back through such Christian exemplars as Alcuin's Conflictus Veris et Hiemis to Ovid, Amores 3.1 and Aristophanes' Frogs. It is a favourite poetic form in the 12th and 13th Centuries, when Latin lyrics incorporate such debates as Wine v Water, Rich Man v Poor Man, Helen v Ganymede (see Manitius, 3.944ff.).

The particular debate between the clericus and the miles as love-suitors becomes popular in the Latin and the vernacular poetry of the 12th and 13th Centuries. Though it is tempting to connect it with the tenzon or poetic debate popular at court, it is important to note that with the exception of Florence and Blancheflor in Anglo-Norman poetry, the cleric invariably prevails in the debate. So it is clear that the authors of Anni parte florida, The Love-Council of Remiremont, and such vernacular poems as Hueline and Anglantine are clerics. Moreover the cleric's superiority is in each case ascribed to his education and knowledge.[2] We are back in the milieu of the schools, where our learned clerical author can exploit Ovid's handling of a similar theme in Amores 3.8. But the tables are turned. The Roman poet bewails the wilful preference accorded by the lady to the soldier over the man of letters; Anni parte florida recounts the victory of learning over the mindless warrior.

The detailed argumentation on the desirable and undesirable qualities of the cleric are closely similar to the remarks of the noblewoman and the reply of the cleric in Andreas Capellanus' De Amore I.6H - the cleric harping on his superior knowledge extending to love-lore and on his generosity, the noblewoman pouring scorn on his clothes, tonsure, and greedy manners. Both poem and treatise should be considered in connexion with The Love-Council of Remiremont (for editions and bibliography see Manitius, 3.565ff.). In 1151 Pope Eugenius III reproached this convent-community for its luxurious ways, and in the poem (presumably inspired by the rebuke) the nuns in council debate the respective merits of clerics and knights as suitors. Those who prefer the knight are finally excommunicated:-

Amor deus omnium	iuventutis gaudium,
clericos amplectitur,	et ab eis regitur.
tales ergo diligo,	stultos quoque negligo.

There has been considerable controversy on which came first, with Walther arguing for the anteriority of The Love-Council and Faral for that of Phyllis and Flora; but neither content nor manuscripts permit a firm judgment, and we must be content with a non liquet.[3]

It may be useful to clarify the canonical position of clerics vis-à-vis love and marriage. A simple cleric was one who had received the tonsure with a view to the religious life, but had not been admitted to minor orders. 'clericatus autem non est ordo, sed quaedam professio vitae dantium se divino ministerio.' (Aquinas, De articulis fidei). He could marry and remain a cleric, and indeed was expected to do so, as Ivo of Chartres makes clear (Decr. 8.286; P.L. 161, 646). So there would be many young clerics living the religious life and wearing the habit and tonsure for whom marriage was not out of the question. But the general tradition had grown up within the western church from the IVth Century onward that those who performed the sacramental liturgy should not marry, so those who took orders were opting for celibacy. Abelard, for example, makes it clear that those above the rank of acolyte are not permitted marriage (Hist. Calam. 5). The evidence of satirical poetry and such treatises as that of Andreas makes it clear that this did not deter all such celibates from the theory or the practice of courtly love.

The poem divides clearly into three sections:-

1   1-11   Scene and disputants
2   12-41   The debate, with three exchanges
          a)   12-14 the suitors named
          b)   15-27 their characters
          c)   28-41 their appearance
3   42-79   The adjudication
          a)   42-43 the choice of adjudicator
          b)   44-59 the journey   45-48 Phyllis' mule
                                         49-52 Flora's horse
                                         53-57 Flora's saddle
                                         58-59 the travellers
          c)   60-71 the court of Cupid
          d)   72-76 the person of Cupid
          e)   77-79 the adjudication

1   The setting is spring, with weather and countryside conspiring to evoke feelings of love.
    dum ML = cum.

111

nuntius Aurore Lucifer, stella Veneris (appropriately).

Phyllidis et Flore For the name Phyllis ('foliage' in Greek) cf. Virg., Ecl. 3.78, Hor., C. 4.11.3; for the name Flora, after the Roman goddess of flowers, Ovid, Fasti 1.595, etc. Their names appear often in the love-lyrics of the C.B. (see the Index to Hilka-Schumann-Bischoff 1.3).

2   et locus i.e. as well as the participants.
      ludum = ἀγών, disputatio.

3   reginae 'noblewomen', even in CL (Mart. 10.64.1). Cf. 4: 'nec stirpe viles.'
      respondent 'shine like'.

4   iuveniles In contemporary Provençal lyrics, the word jovens has quite a different sense from 'youthful', connoting "la réalisation parfaite de l'idéal de cortezia, dont l'élément le plus important est . . . generosité" (Lazar, Amour courtois et fin'amors (Paris 1964), 42). So perhaps also here 'the years and spirit of generous youth'.
      parum ML = paulum, 'somewhat'.
      miles ML = 'knight'.

5   habitus . . . moris Taking up in reverse order intus et foris from the preceding line.

6-7   For the amoenus locus and its features, cf. XXII above (breeze, grass, stream, shady tree).

7   venustata An antique word, revived in Christian Latin by Ambrose and others.

9   longe 'further away'.
      in sese redit 'get their breath back'.

9   alternantur 'change colour'
      furor Used of Dido's passion, Virg., Aen. 4.91, etc.

10   de consimili = consimiliter; cf. de improviso, de integro, etc.
      mutuo rependit 'balance each other'.

11   multum . . . more = morae, 'is slow to unfold'.
      incipit i.e. the contest proper.

12   Paris Frequently the exemplar of the knight in the middle ages; cf. Archpoet, 8.18.4. C.B. 143.3 shows him also as the model for lovers: 'simus iussu Cypridis / gloriantes / et letantes pares esse Paridis'. See also IX 3 above.
      Dionei laris 'of Venus' abode', Venus being the daughter of Dione, but often conflated with her; see 41 n.

13   iacit in obliquum 'glances sideways at her', 'gives her an Irish look.

        poteras dicere Parenthetical.

        mendicum 'a ragamuffin', one of the indigent knights to whom the more fortunate miles was expected to present clothes and other gifts. See Andreas Capellanus I.6H.

14   Alcibiades Used as the soubriquet of the cleric because Socrates' pupil is both handsome and learned.

        iura 'privileges'.

15   virgunculam A form perhaps familiar to the poet from Juvenal 13.40, but popular in the Middle Ages.

        Epicuro ML knows only the debased Epicureanism of Roman letters. Cf. esp. C.B. 211: 'Alte clamat Epicurus / "venter satur est securus / venter deus meus eris" . . . '. The cleric is Epicurean in such contexts because of his reputation for otium and fattening meals.

16   fedo = foedo.

        solum . . . Epicurum 'nothing but an Epicurus'.

        implet latera moles et pinguedo 'his fat bulk bulges round him'. The charge that the cleric is 'a slave to nothing but his belly' is made by Andreas Capellanus' noblewoman (I.6H).

17   a castris Cupidinis This image of service (militiae) to Love, so widespread in medieval literature, goes back to Ovid, Am. 1.9.1, etc.

18   illi The dative is found even in CL after prohibet with accusative of the thing forbidden (here the ne clause).

        iuventus See the note on iuveniles in 4.

19   loro pari 'on equal rein', i.e. 'in the same category'.

        ludere 'love-sport'; cf. X 8 above.

        dare . . . dari Contrasting the largitas of the courtly knight with the clerical student who begs, and later seeks a benefice.

20   haurit . . . sanguinem In CL this would normally mean to 'draw blood from another' (Cic., Sest. 54, Livy 9.1.9). Here Flora 'drains the blood from her modest face', i.e. grows pale with anger.

        secundo For the risus primus, see 13.

        reserat 'opens the door to'.

        artibus With fecundo.

21   acuta 'keen' in argument but also 'strident' in tone.

lilio cicuta i.e. poison prevails over innocence. At Hor., Sat. 2.3.69 and 175 Cicuta ('Hemlock') is the soubriquet of an unsavoury money-lender.

22 Answering the first accusation in 19.

dixisti . . . quod Colloquial and biblical, hence common in ML.

probitas For this as a key-quality of courtliness, see XVI 2 above.

parum patere 'allow me a moment'.

23 The stanza answers the second accusation in 19.

fateor 'I maintain'.

quod . . . incogitat ML = ut incogitet. For the verb cf. Hor., Ep. 2.1.122.

Cereris, Lyei Together in this symbolic sense at Virg., Georg. 2.229.

pocula 'fine goblets'.

24 quod non potest Cf. the note in 23 (quod . . . incogitat); 'so sweet that no words can describe it'.

plaudit alis 'beats applause with his wings'; cf. Ovid, Met. 8.239.

indeficiens Like the resources of the cleric!

25 macer aut afflictus For the lean poverty of some knights, see the next stanza and Andreas Capellanus I.6H.

cui respondet . . . 'and the unfeigned affection of his lady is in harmony with him'.

26 preelectus Postclassical.

causa . . . effectus The language of the schools jocularly used to indicate that lack of means brings lacks of strength.

27 For the theme of poverty and its disastrous effect on love, see Andreas Capellanus, II.3: "A lover preoccupied by severe poverty is troubled by such thoughts about his property and the need oppressing him that he cannot devote himself to deeds of love." One of the signal duties of the lover is to offer help when asked (Andreas, I.6C: "The man who wishes to be considered worthy to serve in Love's army should not be preoccupied with miserliness, but abound in generosity, for he ought to lavish largesse on all he can.").

reditus 'revenues'.

28 utrisque . . . utraque i.e. the knight's and the cleric's.

probabiliter 'persuasively'.

29 lucis feste A Sunday or a feastday, when the cleric attends (and if in major orders celebrates) the liturgy.

in tonsura . . . atra veste The tonsure and the clerical garb are regular points of ridicule. Cf. Andreas I.6H where the noblewoman says: "The cleric appears clad in womanly raiment, his head hideously shorn.".

30   appareat 'is obvious'.

31   Bucephalam . . . Ganymedes Bucephalas, the horse of Alexander the Great, is commonly found as the name of a battle-steed in ML, for the Alexander-theme, as exploited by Curtius and other Latin writers, had a great vogue. Ganymede, the cup-bearer of Jupiter, was an obvious soubriquet for the squire of a knight; the name is used of a boy-favourite, as in the poetic contest between Ganymede and Helen (Manitius 3.947).

32   reiecta 'pushed back'.

33   os ponens in celum 'panegyrising'; cf. Cic., Att. 7.1.5. etc.
      et per acum Cf. Mark 10.25.

34   mel pro felle The mel/ fel jingle, going back all the way to Plautus (Cist. 69: 'amor et melle et felle est fecundissimus') is found in many medieval lyrics.
      probas = approbas.
      ferum = animosum, 'aggressive'. animositas is a necessary quality for a courtly knight. Cf. Andreas 2.1: 'si talis sit amator, cui congruat bellatorem exsistere, studere debet ut eius cunctis appareat animositas manifesta, quia plurimum cuiusque probitati detrahitur, si timidus proeliator exsistat'.
      pauperies sc. makes him aggressive.

35   amplius reclames 'contest too loudly'.
      quibus . . . 'they are the stimulus of his path to death and Hades'; i.e. it is not love that makes him fight and live dangerously, but hunger.

36   multum est . . . 'the knight's adversity is most wearing'.
      in arto Classical; Ovid, Met. 9.683, etc.
      valeat ML = possit.
      requisita Rare but classical, as Quint, 8.6.59.

37   morem 'the convention'.
      ad summum honorem Cf. Andreas I.6H, where the cleric answers the noble lady's argument mentioned in 29. 'Such adornment has been enjoined on me according to the instruction laid down by the ancient wisdom of the fathers, so that clerics may be distinguished from other men in dress and walk . . . '.

38   universa . . . prona 'Clearly the cleric has everything accessible to him'.
      corona The tonsure is the cleric's crown and symbol of authority.

imperat militibus In Andreas the cleric is said to have the highest social status of all because he is chosen by God.

largitur dona Cf. 27 n.

39   celi vias dividit, etc. i.e. he is a student of astronomy and of the physical world.

et rerum naturas In Andreas I.6H the cleric discourses learnedly on the physical differences imposed by nature on men and women. When the woman dismisses such scientific knowledge, he adds: "A knowledge of physics or science generally cannot diminish a man's goodness.".

40   meus . . . lectica Note the function of alliteration and chiasmus in achieving this amusing antithesis.

ubi gesta, etc. In Andreas I.6H, one of the reasons advanced by the cleric for his superiority as suitor over the layman is his 'knowledge of all things'. The gesta principum may well refer to the Lives of Suetonius, the range of whose influence in the 12th Century can be measured by a glance at the Index of Manitius 3.

41   Dione The name of Venus' mother is frequently used for Venus herself by Ovid, Am. 1.14.33, etc. See 12 above.

Cytherus 'a follower of Venus' = CL Cythereius; e.g., Ovid calls Aeneas Cythereius heros (Met. 13.625, etc). The island of Cythera off C. Malea in the Peloponnese was a famous shrine of Venus.

sermo reus 'Your words are indictable on these and such other counts.'.

42   Note that it is Flora the cleric's girl who demands recourse to Cupid for judgment.

examen 'judgment' (ML).

redeunt i.e. to their castle or court.

43   cite . . . utriusque i.e. the cleric's and the knight's.

noverit Subjunctive in oratio obliqua.

45   unus ML = quidam.

quem . . . Neptunus Poseidon/Neptune was held to be creator and tamer of the horse; for his gifts of horses, cf. Claudian, Stil. Cons. III, 265f. I know of no classical passage indicating the gift of a horse to Venus; the motif seems more appropriate to the medieval conception of a gift to a high lady.

post Adonis funus For Venus' infatuation with Adonis, and his death after being wounded by a boar, cf. Ovid, Met. 10.529ff.

Cytheree Venus; see 41 above.

46 probe regine . . . Hiberine 'a noble Spanish lady'. The form Hiberina is found at Juv. 6.53; for regina, cf. 3 n. Phyllis is depicted as the daughter of a Spanish noblewoman presumably married to a French aristocrat.

eo . . . divine 'because she had devoted herself to the work of the goddess'.

opere (from opera) divine is dative.

leto fine 'by a happy outcome'.

47 faciebat nimium 'the mule did a lot for the maiden's appearance'.

habilis Here and in 51 the meaning seems to be 'presentable' rather than 'nimble' or manageable'.

Nereus A sea-god in CL distinct from Neptune (cf. Virg., Aen. 8.383, Ovid, Met. 13.742) is here identified with him.

Dione See 41 n.; the case is dative.

48 superpositis 'trappings'.

quod . . . fuerunt ML = haec omnia talia fuisse.

49 utriusque 'divitiarum et decoris' is to be understood from the preceding line.

50 Pegaseis loris Cf. Claudian, In Ruf. 1.263: 'non Pegaseis adiutus habenis', 'Subdued by the reins of Pegasus' implies that Flora's horse shares Pegasus' qualities.

pictus artificio . . . 'artistically dappled with differing hues'.

nigredini Post-classical and biblical.

51-52 The characteristics of the ideal horse as listed in these two stanzas are a commonplace in antiquity. They all appear in Xenophon's Art of Horsemanship I, 3-12, the only disagreement being that Xenophon believes the shin-bone should not be too upright (contrast 52). In CL there are descriptions in Varro, De agr. 2.7.5, Columella 6.29.2ff., Virg., Georg. 3.72ff; see now P. Vigneron, Le cheval dans l'antiquité (Nancy 1968), 4ff. But the closest comparison with these verses is Isidore, Etym. 12.1.45.

51 respexit . . . . 'its gaze was rather lordly but not savage'.

leve i.e., lēve, 'spread smoothly out'. The adverb is not found in CL.

52 dorso pando, etc. 'along its curved back, the spine, which had not been subjected to burdens, extended for the maiden to sit upon'. iaceo in CL often expresses superimposed physical features. sessure is the dative of the future participle.

pede cavo Cf. Xenophon (n. 51-2 above), 1.4: 'the hollow hoof striking the earth rings like a cymbal'.

tibia recta, largo crure 'straight-shinned, big-shanked'.

totum fuit . . . studium 'showed all Nature's skill'.

53-57 It is an oversimplification to suggest that saddles were unknown in antiquity; see Vigneron (n. 51-52 above), 82ff. But the saddle described here reflects contemporary techniques of saddlery. See Gay, Glossaire archéologique du moyen âge et de la renaissance, s.v. 'selle', where there are relevant illustrations and descriptions from contemporary vernacular literature.

53 radiabat Hilka-Schumann-Bischoff prefers the reading faciebat, governing superposita. radiabat is equally well attested and is supported by enim in the next line.

auri cella 'a gold frame'.

capitella 'raised corners'.

venustavit . . . 'a jewel enhanced each like a star'.

54 The fondness for describing such art-motifs in literature begins with Homer's description of the shield of Achilles (Il. 18.478ff.; see 56 below), and there are many examples in Virgil's Aeneid. In the M.A., interest in symbolism made the device a popular one; so in the Anticlaudianus of Alan of Lille, after the seven liberal Arts construct the parts of a chariot, paintings on each part depict the discipline of the individual creator.

nuptie Mercurii As described in the treatise of Martianus Capella, De nuptiis Philologiae et Mercurii. This work enjoyed a huge popularity in the M.A.

superis admotis See Mart. Cap. 1.97 for the presents of the deities.

dotis See Mart. Cap. 9.892ff., where Philologia's mother Sophia presents a dowry to her daughter.

55 planus 'unadorned'.

illa i.e. multa sculpta from 54.

vix, etc. 'scarcely believed that his hands could have done it'.

56 clipeo Achillis See 54 n.

laboravit phaleras The accusative after the verb in this sense of 'artistically create' is common in Augustan poetry, e.g. Virg., Aen. 1.639.

indulsit 'devoted himself to'.

ferraturam ML = 'horseshoes'.

sponse i.e. Venus.

57 subinsuta bysso 'stitched on with cotton'.

acantho texuerat . . . Minerva had stitched on the design of the acanthus and narcissus. For the acanthus on pottery, cf. Virg., Ecl. 3.45. The two flowers are mentioned in the same line by Virg., Georg. 4.123. Gay (see above, 53 n.) quotes Theophilus, Schedula: 'potes in auro et argento facere bestiolas atque aviculas, ac flores super sellas equestres matronarum.'.

tenas The sense demands a meaning like 'edges'. RMLW offers tenua in the sense of 'fringe' with an obelisk signifying doubt on the form of spelling.

fimbriavit The participle fimbriatus ('fringed') is classical.

58 domicelle ML; 'damsels'.

lilia . . . rose a cliché in poetic descriptions of beautiful complexions; so Alan of Lille, Anticlaudianus 1.281f.: 'sidereum vultus castigavere ruborem / lilia nupta rosis . . .'.

59 ad Amoris, etc. The girls now ride to the estate of Cupid. Similar descriptions of such journeys to folk-lore wonderlands appear in contemporary romances. A most interesting parallel is the description of Cupid's court in Andreas Capellanus I.6E, where the palace is described in detail, followed by an account of how different types of ladies - courtly lovers, those of easy virtue, those who reject all suitors - are treated after death. See also Andreas II. 8, where a knight forces his way into Arthur's court, and finds there the rules for love.

paradisum See XXII 3 above.

dulcis ira 'anger attractively gives life . . . '

accipitrem manu . . . nisum In Andreas II.8, the knight who goes to Arthur's court presents the falcon he obtained there to the lady who had dispatched him. It is doubtful if the poet intends any clear difference between accipiter and nisus (Nisus was the king of Megara who was changed into a sparrow-hawk; cf. Ovid, Met. 8.8f.).

60 pigmentum The word in CL means 'cosmetic', but its sense extends to 'spice' in ML.

tympana cithareque Such disembodied music is characteristic of folk-lore and of such literary stories as that of Cupid and Psyche (Apul., Met. 5.1ff.) developed from it.

61 diatessaron, . . . diapente These Greek terms for kinds of music were known to 12th C. writers through Macrobius, Martianus Capella, and Boethius. Diatessaron literally means 'using four strings'; Macrobius, Comm. in Somn. Scip. 2.1.25, says 'symphonia diatessaron constat de duobus tonis et hemitonio . . . et fit ex epitrito' (i.e. 4:3). Cf. Boethius, De Mus. 1.8: 'quae in numeris

sesquitertia est (i.e. 4:3), diatessaron in sonis.'. diapente means 'using five strings', and is used to express the 3:2 melody. Macrobius says 'diapente constat ex tribus tonis et hemitonio, et fit de hemiolo' (i.e. 3:2). It is perhaps interesting that these terms are found in Alan of Lille, Anticlaudianus 3.436f.

62 symphonia A form of drum. Isidore, Orig 3.22: 'symphonia vulgo appellatur lignum cavum ex utraque pelle extenta, quam virgulis hinc et inde feriunt.'. There is a wealth of information on musical instruments in this section of Isidore.

phiale ML = 'viols'.

buxus 'boxwood pipe'; cf. Virg., Aen. 9.619, Ovid, Met. 4.30.

multiplici . . . via Presumably referring to the holes in the pipe.

63 corydalus The crested lark.

graculus A curious choice as member of the chorus in view of the old proverb 'nihil cum fidibus graculo' (Gell., praef. 19).

philomena See XIV 4 n. above.

de transacta pena 'about the pains she had suffered'. She was violated by her brother-in-law Tereus and her tongue cut out so that she could not inform her sister (Ovid, Met. 6.450ff.).

64 coniectatur . . . thalamus 'they guess that this is the abode . . . '. thalamus, marriage chamber, is the appropriate word for Cupid's lodging.

65 modico timore 'a little apprehensively'.

crescunt in amore i.e. under the influence of Cupid's person and retinue.

66 fraglant This alternative form of fragrant, frequent from the time of Apuleius, seems much preferable to the flagrant of the mss, retained by Hilka-Schumann-Bischoff.

67 domicellarum See 58 n.

capiuntur 'entranced'.

68 cantilene In the good sense of 'harmonious song', common both in classical and biblical Latin.

vene 'hearts' or perhaps 'blood'.

69 Fauni, Nymphe, Satyri Cf. VIII 3 n above.

comitatus multus In apposition, 'a numerous escort'.

tympanizant A classical word; cf. Suet., Aug. 68.

70 sed Silenus titubat A clear reminiscence of Ovid, Met. 11.89ff.: 'Hunc assueta

cohors Satyri Bacchaeque frequentant; / at Silenus abest. titubantem annisque
meroque / ruricolae cepere Phryges .. . '.

71   somno vergit 'sways through dozing'.

asino prevectus i.e. 'riding by'. Cf. Ovid, A.A. 1.543f.: 'Ebrius ecce senex
pando Silenus asello / vix sedet . . . '. Cf. also Fasti 1.399t.

dei i.e. Bacchus; 'causes Bacchus' breast to dissolve in floods of laughter'.

vina The plural is common in Augustan poets.

clamor i.e. Silenus'.

72   sidereus 'glittering'; the word is found with reference to the countenance of
Bacchus at Sen., Oed. 409.

vertex 'the top of his body'.

leva Nominative, as latus shows.

satis Take with potens et elatus.

potest conici 'one can hazard that he is . . . '.

elatus 'august', 'proud', as often in Cicero.

73   floribus perplexo 'wreathed with flowers'.

de capillo pexo Cf. Juv. 11.150.

digito connexo 'their fingers interlocked'.

74   tute (nom.) 'unthreatened'.

venerabili . . . iuventute This is the traditional Greek vision of Cupid. Cf.
Longus, 2.3ff., where the young boy is 'older than Saturn and all that is'.

cinctum 'adorned', as often in classical poetry.

virtute 'powerful presence', the biblical force of the word.

prevenit salute 'greeted them first', like the courtly deity he is.

75   parum pausa 'rest a while'. parum = ML for paulum. pausa was familiar to the
poet from such biblical contexts as 4 Esdras (now relegated to the Apocrypha),
2.24: 'pausa et requiesce, populus meus'.

res . . . clausa 'this unsolved problem'.

76   retractari etc. Perhaps in 76 this is just as well.

expresse 'unambiguously'.

77   iudices . . . iura The so-called courts of love were taken seriously by many
19th-Century scholars, but today they are generally regarded as at most
occasions of social amusement, if they existed at all.

Usus et Natura The idea expressed here is the commonplace one that habit as
well as natural attraction is powerful in love. Cf. Apuleius, Met. 5.4.5. For

usus or consuetudo in this role, cf. Lucr. 4.1283, 'consuetudo concinnat amorem'; Ovid, A.A. 2.345. For natura, cf. Cic., Fin. 3.62, and the definition of love in Andreas Capellanus, 1.1.: 'amor est passio quaedam innata . . . '.

curie censura 'the judgment of the court'.

78   ventilant vigorem 'they give rein to the power of justice'.

rigorem cf. iustitie (curie being dative).

secundum scientiam 'in virtue of his knowledge'; see the introductory comment to this poem.

ad amorem Cf. C.B. 82, refl.: 'clerus scit diligere virginem plus milite'.

79   futuris 'in future'. For the neuter plural, cf. 77 above.

fatentur pluris 'claim he is of greater worth'.

Notes

1   Cf. E. Faye Wilson, Speculum (1948), 35ff., who suggests that a common pattern in the epithalamium - conversation in heaven, journey of Venus to earth, marriage in bride's home - is artistically inverted with the conversation on earth followed by the journey to the heaven where Cupid dwells.

2   Cf. W.T.H. Jackson, Z.F.D.A. (1954), 253ff.

3   For further detail and bibliography see H. Walther, Das Streitgedicht in des lateinisches Literatur des Mittelalters (Munich 1920), 147; E. Faral, Recherches sur les sources latines des contes et romans du moyen age (Paris 1913), 191ff.

XXIV Ecce torpet

(Of the four mss besides B in which this piece appears, C is at Cambridge (Corp. Chr. 450, 14th Century) and O at Oxford (Bodl. Add. A.44)).

This poem, the first of three satirical pieces confidently ascribed to Walter of Châtillon, laments the decay of worthy manners as manifest in two particular ways - the decay of generous giving and indifference to one's plighted word. As always with Walter's poems, the structure reflects the theme with clarity. The first stanza states the two themes of miserliness and deceit; the second pinpoints the basic cause of avaritia; the third and fourth dilate on the two sins separately; and the final stanza reflects on the subhuman manner of life which they create. As often, Walter achieves his message primarily through the techniques of paradox and oxymoron, prominent especially in the first and final stanzas.

1   As always, Walter shows himself influenced by the Roman satirists; Juvenal harps on the decay of probitas (1.74: 'probitas laudatur et alget'). It is a favourite theme of Walter's - cf. Mor.-sat. Ged. 10: 'captivata largitas longe relegatur / exulansque probitas misere fugatur / dum virtuti pravitas prave novercatur.'.

largitas On the prominence of this virtue in medieval lyric, cf. Dronke, 199.

parcitas largitur 'Niggardliness is freely given'.

verum dicit. etc. i.e. in the topsy-turvy world, falsehood and truth have reversed their roles, and the false is regarded as the true.

(Refl.) omnes iura ledunt appears also in Walter Map, 172.43.

res illicitas Biblical: cf. Gen. 34.7, Lev. 20-21.

licite Their injustice is legitimised, and this is the basis of Walter's complaint.

2   quivis 'anyone you can mention' (= quiviscunque).

censu 'wealth', the sense common in Horatian satire.

(Refl.) quelibet 'any you can name'.

3   do das dedi, etc. Such playful exploitation of paradigms, as a means of laying emphasis on a virtue like largitas, is found in the Archpoet, 6.42, 'verbum laudabile do das'; and also in Mor.-sat. Ged. 10.3.1: 'quondam diffusissimum verbum do das dedi, / nunc est angustissimum . . .' etc.

mari comparare Eccle. 1.7 offers the clue: 'bene et recte cor avari mari comparatur, quia sicut de mari sacra scriptura veraciter dicit quod omnia flumina intrant in mare et mare non redundat (se Eccle. 1.7), ita et eadem loquitur de avaro, quod avarus non impletur pecunia' (Distinctiones monasticae, quoted by Hilka-Schumann-Bischoff).

(Refl.) et . . . excedunt 'in calculating their possessions they get beyond counting', i.e. they have so much they can't count it.

4   perit fides Cf. Jer. 7.28: 'periit fides et ablata est de ore eorum.'.

nullus fidus fido 'none is faithful to a faithful companion'.

nec Iunoni Iupiter Referring to his marital infidelities as described in Ovid's Metamorphoses.

Enee Dido Reversing the Virgilian pattern, in which Aeneas was faithless to Dido. The Dido theme has a special group of poems in the C.B., nos. 98ff.

(Refl.) devia 'perverted', a regular sense in CL.

5   (Refl.) quolibet Cf. 2 Refl.

excedunt 'transgress', 'break their word'.

XXV Propter Sion

(The poem is found in a dozen other mss, six of them in the Bodleian. The order of the stanzas is confused in B; see Hilka-Schumann-Bischoff I.1, 69.)

This satirical poem of Walter of Châtillon (Introduction, p. 6), composed about 1171-5 (stanza 27 n.), takes as its theme a lament for Rome. It is composed in the metre frequently exploited for the Sequence (cf. 'Stabat Mater dolorosa / iuxta crucem lacrimosa / dum pendebat filius'). The structure is clear:-

1-2	Lament for Rome
3-25	Dangers of the sea

	3-5	the dangers assembled
	6-8	bithalassus (= 'Franco')
	9-10	hounds of Scylla (= lawyers of the Curia)
	11-12	Charybdis (= the papal chancery)
	13-18	Sirens (= cardinals)
	19-23	Pirates aboard Peter's barque (= cardinals)
	24-25	The rocks (= ianitores)

26-29	The harbours (= Peter of Pavia/Alexander III)
30	A time for silence.

The main preoccupation of the poem is the venality and corruption of the Roman Curia in its dealings with visiting clerics. Since all benefices of any importance had to be ratified at Rome, there were frequently large numbers of clerks requesting such ratification. Set preliminaries were required for such applications and members of the Curia demanded fees for composing the necessary letters.

1   Propter Sion   As so often in medieval poetry, the first stanza evokes a
      scriptural passage which indicates the theme. Isa. 62.1: 'Propter Sion non
      tacebo, et propter Ierusalem non quiescam, donec egrediatur ut splendor iustus
      eius et salvator eius ut lampas accendatur.' Sion is the heavenly city,
      represented on earth by the Church.
      ruinas Rome   For the 4th-C. Christian humanists, pagan Rome was the Babylon
      to be contrasted with Jerusalem. But it is now the centre of Christendom, and
      should be the Jerusalem on earth, which is why Walter laments its moral ruin.
      et ut lampas . . . iustus   Walter skilfully combines the two similes of Isaiah
      quoted above, the knowledge of which he could presume in his readers: 'until . .
      a just man blazes forth like a torch in the Church.' For iustitia . . . oriatur, cf.
      Isa. 45.8.

2   princeps . . . tributo Again the scriptural evocation./ <u>Thren</u> 1.1: 'princeps provinciarum facta est sub tributo'; 1.11: 'vide . . . quoniam facta sum vilis.' It is Rome which is <u>princeps</u>, the chief city of the Church.

quod solebam dicere Indicating earlier satirical poems by Walter on the same theme.

derelictam Cf. <u>Isa</u>. 62.4: 'non vocaberis ultra Derelicta, et terra tua non vocabitur amplius Desolata.'.

opere 'in fact'. For Walter's visit to Rome, see Raby, <u>S.L.P</u>. 2, 190.

3   vidi, vidi Cf. <u>Acts</u> 7.34: 'videns vidi afflictionem populi mei . . . '.

caput mundi So also Lucan 2.136 and 655 of Rome.

instar, etc. 'like the sea, the devouring maw of the Sicilian deep'.

Siculi i.e. <u>freti</u>, with reference to Scylla and Charybdis; cf. Ovid, <u>Met</u>. 7.63ff.

bithalassus Biblical, literally 'the meeting of the seas'; cf. <u>Acts</u> 27.41: 'cum incidissemus in locum bithalassum' (a shoal, the hazard of a sandbank). Cf. also Rufinus, <u>Ep. Clem</u>. 14: 'bithalassa loca, quae duplicibus undae fallacis aestibus verberantur'. Translate: 'The treacherous waters'.

sorbet aurum Crassus In reference to the legend that gathered round the Parthian victory at Carrhae, after which the victors were said to have marked Crassus' cupidity by pouring liquid gold into his dead mouth. Florus 1.46.11: 'aurum enim liquidum in rictum oris infusum est, ut qui arserat auri cupiditate, eius etiam mortuum et exsangue corpus auro ureretur.'. Cf. also Festus, <u>Brev</u>. 17.

4   latrat Because hounds attend her.

Scylla, etc. Cf. Ovid, <u>Met</u>. 14.52ff., Virg., <u>Aen</u> 3.424ff., etc.

galearum In ML, <u>galea</u> = <u>genus navigii velocissimi</u> (Du Cange), often used by pirates.

piratarum Cf. 19 below.

5   Syrtes Here with the general sense of sandbanks which are a hazard to the sailor, rather than the two African Syrtes, Maior and Minor (The Gulfs of Sidra and Cabes). The word was in classical times extended to the metaphorical sense of hazard; e.g., Cic., <u>De Or</u>. 3.163.

Sirenes Here associated with the sandbanks - an original touch. The Homeric Sirens were exploited by the early Fathers as an image of the alluring vices of the world seeking to seduce the dedicated Christian. Cf., after Ovid, <u>Met</u>. 5.557ff., Ambrose, <u>Expos. Psalm</u>, 43, 75: Jerome, <u>Ep</u>. 22.18: Paulinus of Nola,

Ep. 16.7, etc.; and H. Rahner, Greek Myths and Christian Mystery (London 1962), ch. 7.

os humanum Continuing with the image of the Sirens, with their externals of kindly humanity and their inner diabolical nature.

demonium Scriptural (Ps. 95.5, Deut. 32.17) and occasionally elsewhere (Manil. 2.938).

6   iuxta rationem 'in any reasonable view'.

Franconem 'ein fingierter Name' (Strecker). The mss RW read tremonem; but Arundel 26, Si quis dicit, Roma vale, (ed. W. Meyer, Die Arundel Sammlung, 48) has likewise an allusion to the mysterious Franco, one of the denizens of the Curia.

duplex mare Continuing the theme of bithalassus (3 n.).

valens obolum 'a genuine ha'penny'.

7   fluctus The reading of P, is to be preferred to venti from the evidence of Isidore 13.10.4: 'Cani(?) nis succinctam (sc. Scyllam) capitibus, quia collisi ibi fluctus latratus videntur exprimere.'

byssus . . . purpure Cf. Exod. 25.4; Luke 16.19: 'qui induebatur purpura et bysso.'

sepelitur Ps. 13.3: 'sepulcrum patens est guttur eorum'. Cf. Rom. 3.13.

8   illuc enim Cf. Ps. 121.4: 'illuc enim ascenderunt tribus, tribus domini.'

9   canes Scylle Cf. Ovid, Met. 14.59ff.

advocati curie 'the lawyers of the Papal Court'.

pecunie Genitive. 'Sink and destroy the money-laden bark'.

10   iste . . . ille . . . hic The individual advocates of 9.

legistam . . . decretistam Secular and canon lawyers respectively.

inducens 'citing'.

Gelasium Pope 492-6, whose letters include numerous instructions on matters of discipline. But the influential decretum Gelasianum is now considered a 6th-C. compilation.

intendit actionem 'brings on action', a legal expression; cf. TLL 1.442; Cic., Mil. 14).

regundorum finium Note the legal form regundorum - the phrase is used at Cod. Just. 3.39 (cf. Cic., Leg. 1.55, Mur. 22) for 'marking the limits', 'drawing the boundaries of disputed territories.

11   debacchatur 'rages uncontrolled', used of fire by Hor., C. 3.3.55.

cancellaria The Papal Chancery, a sub-division of the Curia, was headed by a cardinal, responsible for Papal rescripts and accordingly exposed to considerable dangers of bribery and corruption. See C.R. Cheney, The Study of the Medieval Papal Chancery (1966).

nemo gratus gratis 'none are welcome without payment'.

neque datur absque datis 'is not given without gifts': cf. C.B. 1.5: 'date vobis dabitur.'

Gratiani gratia The sequence of punning continues with this reference to Gratian, the 12th-C. author of the Decretum which is the basis of canon law. It contains patristic texts, conciliar decrees and papal edicts, together with a commentary (see P.L. 187). The pun was also exploited with reference to St. Gratian; cf. Adam of St. Victor (ed. Gautier, no. 82): 'Gratiani grata sollemnitas / nos ad laudes invitat debitas; / Gratianus laudis materia /multiformi redundat gratia'.

12 plumbum i.e. the lead with which papal edicts were sealed.

informatur 'fashioned' a poetic use in CL.

equitatis . . . plumbeam equitatis fantasia = simulata aequitas, almost 'a travesty of justice'. teste Zacharia is in reference to Zach. 5.7f.: 'et ecce talentum plumbi portabatur, et ecce mulier una sedens in medio amphorae. et dixit: haec est impietas. et proiecit eam in medio amphorae, et misit massam plumbeam in os eius' (sc. amphorae). So the woman in the jar in Zacharias is pushed beneath this lead cover. Herkenrath accordingly proposed to read here supter for super. But cf. Clavis Melitonis, Spic. Solesm. 2.291: 'vidi iniquitatem. super talentum plumbeum', so that the reference is to the earlier situation of the Old Testament passage. The papal bull had the name of the pope on one side, and the heads of Peter and Paul on the obverse, which might explain 'the appearance of justice' in line 4.

13 Syrtes See 5.

byzantium The byzantius was a gold coin deriving its name from the imperial connexion with Byzantium.

parcitatis Preferred to avaritia because of the alliteration.

procella The metaphor of the sea is continued; the Sirens promise smooth waters (lenitatis) but upturn the purse with a storm.

supinant marsupium Note the splendid verbal play. The verb indicates the turning upside down of the purse to disgorge the contents.

14 The cardinals initially address the visitor kindly in his native language, as part of the softening-up process appropriate to Sirens.

15   terra, etc. The poem was composed during the period 1171-5, when the schism of 1159-77 (caused by the emperor Frederick Barbarossa's support of an antipope Victor IV) was in progress. Accordingly the pope, Alexander III, spent a considerable part of his reign in France. (For the date of the poem, see 27 n.) concilii Either the Council of Montpellier (1162) or of Tours (1163).

speciales filii The title which French Catholics continue to claim to this day. Cf. Stephen of Tournai (ed. Desilve no. 63) 'speciales filii Romanae ecclesiae dicimur'.

16   Petri leges Cf. Matt. 16.19.

manicis ferreis Cf. Ps. 149.8: 'ad alligandos reges eorum in compedibus, et nobiles eorum in manicis ferreis.'

17   cardinales / di carnales Splendidly savage word-play.

fel draconis Cf. Deut. 32.33: 'fel draconum'.

in fine lectionis 'at the end of the reading', with an amusing play on the liturgical sequence of gospel followed by the offertory-collection.

bursam vomere Having poured in the poison (line 4), the cardinals force vomiting to follow, but it is the visitor's purse that is emptied! bursam is here the subject of vomere; cf. Lehmann, Par. Texte, no. 19.47f.: 'bursa tua, quae vomuerat, praegnans est.'

18   Crucifixi patrimonium 'the inheritance of Christ crucified' is the technical phrase for the Church's possessions; see Latham, R.M.L.W., patrimonium.

Nero is perhaps the commonest figure for the perfidious tyrant in 12th-C. literature. Cf. Mor.-sat.Ged. 16, 17: Alan of Lille, Anticl. 1.171, 8.208, etc.

intus lupi Cf. Matt. 7.15: 'attendite a falsis prophetis, qui veniunt ad vos in vestimentis ovium, intrinsecus autem sunt lupi rapaces.'

agni ovium Cf. Ps. 113.4 and 6: Eccli. 47.3.

19   Petri navem i.e. the Church; cf. C.B. 53, etc.

clavem, etc. Cf. Matt 16.19: 'et tibi dabo claves regni coelorum, et quod-cumque ligaveris super terram, erit ligatum et in coelis.'

nox nocti Ps. 18.3: 'nox nocti indicat scientiam'. The message of this psalm (Coeli enarrant gloriam dei) is distorted to convey this suggestion of the blind leading the blind.

20   in galea The navis of the previous stanza is now a pirate vessel.

lues inportuna . . . 'The churlish plague of the world'; this is spurius of 21.

camelos deglutiens Cf. Matt. 23.24: 'camelum . . . glutientes'.

canopeo The word in classical poetry means a mosquito-net (Hor., Epod. 9.16, Prop. 3.11.45, Juv. 6.80), but in ML means more generally a canopy.

leo rapiens et rugiens Ps. 21.14: Ezech. 22.25; since the lion symbolises the devil, Spurius is Satanic.

21   In this stanza the cardinals change from sirens to pirates!

Spurius This reading of B ('The Bastard') was not specific enough for many scribes, who insert variants, including Joannes and Pilatus. But as with Franco (6), Spurius is obviously a thinly-veiled pseudonym for a leading prelate.

sedens in insidiis Ps. 10.8: 'sedet in insidiis'.

lata cute 'with expansive flesh', perhaps a play on Juv. 6.464, 'lota cute'.

monstrum nec . . . redemptum An evocation of Juv. 4.2f.: 'monstrum nulla virtute redemptum / a vitiis', a description of another voluptuary, Crispinus.

22   **Achillea** An adjective in place of the genitive Achillis.

sepe legimus Above all in Ovid, Met. 11.221ff. and in the Odes of Horace: Catullus 64 would be less familiar.

sterlingorum The variants carlinorum (N) and ducatorum (K) are ruled out because these coins are not in currency till later in the 13th C. The denarius sterlingus was English but much used in 12th-C. France. For possible etymologies of the word, cf. Du Cange 3.319f.

sancta 'chaste'.

Bursam i.e. the papal purse.

23   **pregnat** Cf. 17 n; 'the papal purse bulges'.

detumescit Of subsiding waters in Statius, Theb. 3.259, 5.468.

24   **rati** The pirates lie waiting in ambush under Spurius (21) for the barque of the Church. It is not clear who the ductor ratis is; not the Pope (see 28).

privati 'stripped of'.

cantator . . . latronibus Cf. Juv. 10.22, 'cantabit vacuus coram latrone viator', a favourite passage of a favourite author for 12th-C. poets.

25   **ianitores** For complaints about ianitores in other contexts, see the amusing account of Matthew Paris on riots at Oxford in Chron. Maiora (Rolls ed. 3.484ff.); also C.B. 42.11.

pauper . . . .et egenus Cf. Job 24.14; Ps. 35.10, 69.6.

26   **applicari** The word artistically covers both the movement of the ship to the safety of the island and the 'application' for fair treatment to Peter or Alexander.

iacturam 'damage' to the boat, but also 'loss' sustained by the visitor.

27 Petrus Papiensis Peter of Pavia, one of the two 'harbours', became cardinal bishop of Frascati in 1179.

Meldensis He was named bishop of Meaux in 1171 but not consecrated by Alexander III till 1175; see J.M. Brixius, Die Mitglieder des Kardinalkollegiums von 1130-1181 (diss. Berlin 1912), p. 65, no. 23, p. 124, no. 168. Hence this poem was written between 1171 and 1175.

28 fetus ager Cf. Ovid, Fasti 1.662.

florens ortus i.e. hortus. Cf. Anal. Hymn. 45, 99.11: 'florens hortus austro flante / hortus fetus balsamo'.

Alexander . . . meus i.e. Pope Alexander III (1159-81), whose behaviour is thus sharply distinguished from the avarice of his Curia. It is clear that Walter is on terms of intimacy with him.

29 ille fovet litteratos For Alexander's academic career and interests (as canon lawyer, theologian, philosopher), see D.T.C. 1. 711ff. His letters are in P.L. 200.

latus Elisaei Giezi corrumperet Cf. 4 Kings 5.20ff., where Eliseus cured Naaman of leprosy, and Eliseus' servant Giezi tried to exploit the cure for his own advantage, but was visited with the leprosy which Naaman had cast off. So here Alexander would be a true Eliseus 'if Giezi were not corrupting his flank'; i.e. if he were not compromised by venal associates in the Curia.

30 naufragari Cf. Anal. Hymn. 21, 204.5: 'ex quo Romam veneris / nisi te nudaveris / vix absolvi poteris / curiae naufragiis.'

dum securus eo For the implication, see 24 n.

ori . . . custodiam Cf. Ps. 38.2: 'posui ori meo custodiam'.

XXVI Versa est in luctum

(The poem is found only in B).

We have already seen in Propter Sion how the author of this poem, Walter of Châtillon, subtly exploits an image (the perils of the sea) derived from nature and developed from classical mythology to describe the corruption of the Roman Curia. The object of attack in this poem is likewise the leadership of the Church, and Walter here sustains the different image of mountains and valleys as representing leaders and laity. This sustained imagery is all the more effective because the mountain is familiar to students of scripture as one of the most pervasive of the biblical images which the Fathers exploited as a type of the saint.

The structure of Walter's poem, as always, is a model of clarity:-

1	Cause of lamentation
2	Valleys and mountains in shadow
3	The valleys explained
4	The mountains explained
5	The vices of the mountains
6	Prayer for the end of this corrupt era.

1   Versa est in luctum Note as in XXV a scriptural exordium. Cf. Job 30.31: 'versa est in luctum cithara mea', so that we are meant to visualise Walter as a Job tempted to despair. But with the characteristic synthesis of biblical and classical evocations, Walter may also intend us to recall Hor., C. 1.24.2ff: 'praecipe lugubris / cantus, Melpomene, cui liquidam pater / vocem cum cithara dedit.'

non quia se ductum, etc. We have no further information about this laicisation, except perhaps John of Salisbury, Ep. 195: 'doleo Christi regis sigillum esse subtractum . . . '.

abiecti . . . morbi 'of his degrading disease'; a reference to the leprosy of Walter's later years;   John of Garland wrote: 'Magister Gualterius, qui composuit Alexandreida, cum percuteretur a lepra, dixit "Versa est in luctum cythara mea".'. See Manitius, 3.921 n. 1; Raby, S.L.P. 2.203.

(Refl.) So Mor.-sat. Ged. 7.10: 'si verum subtilius libet intueri'.

2   In the Fathers, the trees and mountains of the Old and New Testaments are allegorised and become the saints and leaders of the Church. The 'goodly black firs' of 3 Kings 5.8 are the holy men of the mountain which is the Church (see Paulinus of Nola, Ep. 23.29); it is on the mountain that the light must shine before all men (Matt. 5.14).

132

The image is of the evening gloaming after sunset, when the valleys lose the light first, and the darkness gradually embraces the hills.

proximo Adverb.

nec fallis nec falleris Cf. C.B. 117.11: 'nisi fallar, non falleris'.

3   exleges 'lawless'; cf. Hor., A.P. 224, etc.

notos turpi nota 'stamped with the stigma of infamy'. At Rome when the censors censured an individual for immorality, they affixed the nota censoria to his name on the roll.

principes et reges In apposition to laicos, will refer to Henry II of England. See Introduction p. 3).

luxus et ambitio Combined at Lucan 4.817: 'ambitus et luxus'; cf. Mor.-sat. Ged. 5.21.4.

quasi nox Sustaining the image.

bisacuto Post-classical: see Du Cange ad loc.

4   fontes I adopt Strecker's semicolon after fontes, with no stop after sacerdotes. 'It remains for you to interpret the fount of scriptures allegorically so far as the mountains are concerned.'

mystice 'mystically' here = 'allegorically'; cf. Ambrose, In Luc. 7.9, etc.

in vertice Sion Cf. Ps. 2.6: 'ego autem constitutus sum rex ab eo super Sion, montem sanctum eius . . .'. The Fathers interpret Sion as the Church; see XXV 1 n.

pro speculo i.e. a mirror of the Church to the world.

oraculo legis 'the tabernacle of the Law'; cf. Exod. 37.8; 3 Kings 8.6.

5   iubent . . . fenum i.e. the dignitaries of the Church (nostri colles) demean their charges as cattle. Cf. Dan. 4.22: 'eicient te ab hominibus, et cum bestiis ferisque erit habitatio tua; et fenum ut bos comedes.'

molles In the double sense of effeminate luxury and youthfulness.

sanctuarium Biblical; cf. Dan. 8.13, etc.

ad Christi dotes 'for Christ's dowry'; we are to think here especially of the benefices and ecclesiastical positions for which there was such intense lobbying at the Curia.

expertes . . . nepotes 'the ignorant nephews of bishops'; or perhaps nepotes is used in its wider sense of favourites. Cf. Mor.-sat. Ged. 4.6: 'ecce sponsi comites / vendunt sponse dotes.'

(Refl.) si rem bene notes So also Mor.-sat. Ged. 4.6.3.

6 iubileus The 'jubilee year' described at <u>Lev</u>. 25.10ff.: 'revertetur homo ad possessionem suam et unusquisque rediet ad familiam pristinam, quia iubileus est.'. Walter uses the image of return at the jubilee to denote the day when he will return to his <u>patria</u> in heaven.

moriar ne 'May I die to avoid seeing . . . '.

<u>Antichristi frameam</u> Probably 'sword' here, as in the Vulgate at <u>Ps</u>. 16.13. The notion of the Antichrist, the prince of Christ's enemies, begins with the letters of St. John (cf. 1.2.18, etc.) and it is frequently applied to Roman persecutors like Nero. The label is often attached in the 12th C. to those responsible for abuses within the Church.

<u>precessores</u> 'whose high priests'; cf. <u>Luke</u> 22.26.

<u>in Monte Chrismatis</u> The 'annointed mountain' is Sion (see 4), interpreted as the Church.

<u>censuum censores</u> 'reviewing the level of men's riches'.

XXVII Licet eger

(This poem appears in a dozen mss, including Arundel 384 and Cotton Jul. D VII (both in the British Library), Oxford Bodl. Add. A 44, and Cambridge Univ. FF I 17. Only B and C (the Cambridge ms) contain the full eight stanzas printed in the text, and C has the second half in the order 7, 5, 6, 8. The order here is that of B).

This poem, perhaps the most famous of the satirical pieces of Walter of Châtillon, laments the twin vices of the presides ecclesie - avaritia, in its peculiar ecclesiastical form of simony, and the libido of aging clerics. After the introductory stanza, stanzas 2-4 describe the first sin, stanzas 5-6 the second, and stanzas 7-8 combine the two in summary condemnation.

1   eger cum egrotis Walter identifies his own weaknesses with those of the society he criticises. For the biblical word-play, cf. Rom. 12.15, etc.

fungar . . . vice cotis He himself cannot cure the situation, but he can sharpen the blade of another; for the writer as whetstone, cf. Hor., A.P. 304: 'fungar vice cotis, acutum / reddere quae ferrum valet, exsors ipse secandi.'. The Horatian image is taken over again by Walter at Mor.-sat. Ged. 9.13: 'cum secare nequeam, fungar vice cotis; / imitantur presules Christum a remotis.'.

ius sacerdotis He arrogates the priest's right by denouncing sin; the phrase is biblical, Lev. 27.21.

Sion filie Christ's words at Luke 23.28 ('Weep, daughters of Jerusalem, not for me but for yourselves and for your children') are applied to the new daughters of Jerusalem, the members of the Church.

imitantur . . . Christum Cf. Eph 5.1: 'estote imitatores Dei . . . '.

a remotis The sense is clear: 'from afar', i.e. 'they are far from imitating Christ'. Editors suggest that the expression is derived from such phrases in philosophical logic as a priori, a posteriori. But cf. Sen., Q.N. 3.26.1: in remoto; Caes., B.G. 1.31.14: 'sedes remotas a Germanis'.

2   privata . . . vita 'without a benefice', taking sacerdos / levita as subject with degens.

sacerdos vel levita 'priest or deacon'; cf. I. 1.

via trita Again biblical; cf. Num. 20.19.

Simonis auspicio See Acts 8.18ff., where Simon offers the apostles money in return for their power of laying on hands, and Peter replies: 'Keep your money to perish with you, because you have thought that the gift of God may be bought with money.'. Hence our word simony. Translate: 'following the example of Simon'.

cui i.e. cum eo, cui.

datio In the technical classical sense of 'right of disposal'; cf. Livy 39.19.5.

Giezita 'Simonist'; cf. 4 Kings 5.20ff., where Giezi took money from Naaman when Naaman was cured of leprosy, and as a result was himself struck down with the disease. Cf. Omer 351, 14.4.2, 'regnant Gyezite'.

3 iacet 'is in low estimation'.

sponsa Christi i.e. the Church.

generosa generalis i.e. a meretrix, 'a prostitute lavish with her favours'.

cum, etc. 'though the grace on sale is of small value'.

4 donum dei Eccle. 3.13, etc.

qui vendit Cf. Mor.-sat. Ged. 5.17: 'qui ecclesiam vendunt et mercantur'.

lepra Syri Naaman (see 2 n.) was a Syrian; cf. 4 Kings 5.27: 'lepra Naaman adhaerebit tibi' (sc. Giezi).

ambitus Here = avaritia. Cf. Eph. 5.5: 'avarus, quod est idolorum servitus'. Translate: 'The one whom such greed, which is slavery to idols, encompasses, is not joined to the temple of the Holy Spirit.'.

compaginatur Cf. Augustine, Contra Faustum 6.9: 'tabernaculo . . . Dei, quod est ecclesia, non compaginari . . . peccatum est.'. For templo sancti Spiritus, cf. 1 Cor. 6.19, etc.

5 tenorem 'Manner of life'.

pastorem I punctuate thus. The first two lines look backward, the others forward.

renum i.e. the seat of the passions. Cf. Mor.-sat. Ged. 8.10.2: Apoc. Gol. 99.4, etc.

sanguisuge filia Cf. Prov. 30.15: 'sanguisuge (= leech) duae sunt filiae dicentes: Affer, affer.'. The second daughter after avaritia is libido or luxuria.

duxit in uxorem Cf. Political Songs of England, ed. T. Wright (London 1839), 225.1: 'hoc facit pecunia, / quam omnis fere curia / iam duxit in uxorem.'.

venalis curia Cf. C.B. 4.2.6, etc.

6 in diebus Cf. Eccle. 12.1: 'memento Creatoris tui in diebus iuventutis tuae, antequam appropinquent anni de quibus dicas "non mihi placent".'.

medium i.e. virtutem. In scholastic philosophy, as in the Aristotelian philosophy inspiring it, the medium is the virtue between the extremes, which are its opposite vices; e.g., courage is the virtue between the opposites of cowardice and foolhardiness. In their anxiety to avoid the rigours of old age, the clerics seek the mean between _senectus_ and _iuventus_, but in so doing fall into the vice common to youth.

7   _inamenum_ So also Ovid, _Met_. 10.15.

    sanctum chrisma Cf. _Mor.-sat. Ged_. 9.5.3: 'sacrum vendunt chrisma'.

    iuvenantur The verb is found in Horace (_A.P_. 246).

    nec refrenant The phrase is echoed in a poem in _Mor.-sat. Ged_.: 'habentes in capite canos senectutis, / retinent in renibus flores iuventutis.'.

    quasi modo geniti Cf. the Introit of Low Sunday (In Albis): 'quasi modo geniti infantes, alleluia, rationabile sine dolo lac concupiscite.'.

8   _castitatis . . . murus_ Recalling the biblical image of the _hortus conclusus_, symbolising here the virginity of clerics.

    Epicurus Often in the _C.B_. denoting the prodigal life of _voluptas_; see XXIII 16 describing the cleric.

    nec spectatur moriturus 'One's future death is forgotten'.

    pontifex futurus 'the would-be bishop'.

(There are eight mss besides B which contain this poem, including two at Cambridge (Corpus Christi Coll. 202 (14th Century) and Jesus College 18 (14th/15th Centuries)) and one at Oxford (Rawlinson C 510, 13th Century))

This subtly satirical address to an acquaintance with an abundance of the world's goods bids him exercise restraint and discretion in dispensing them. The tone is deliberately scholastic. There is a mean between miserliness and prodigality at which he must aim: he must investigate carefully the deserving qualities of the recipient. Giving to the undeserving is not an absolute good but only a secondary one, and a reputation for generosity depends on the recipient's being suitable! The origins of this doctrine lie in Aristotle's discussion of the liberal man; cf. <u>Nicomachean Ethics</u>, 4.1: 'Liberality seems to be the mean in relation to wealth . . . prodigality and meanness are excess and deficiency in relation to it . . . the liberal man will give to the right people the right amount at the right time.'. It is the scrupulous adhesion to this doctrine which allows the rich man to remain rich and the poor man to remain poor (stanza 5).

Schreiber suggests that the author of this poem is Walter of Châtillon, but the stylistic criteria are inconclusive.

1   <u>Fas et Nefas</u>   This notion of the proximity of right and wrong is carried over from the classical period (cf. Hor., <u>C</u>. 1.18.10 and Virg., <u>Georg</u>. 1.505) and the first two lines of this poem are echoed in <u>Political Songs of England</u> 48.11, except that <u>casu pari</u> is read there.

<u>passu pari</u>   Cf. Walter of Châtillon, <u>Mor.-sat. Ged.</u> 19.9: 'munus et petitio currunt passu pari'.

<u>redimit</u>   'make good'. The <u>prodigus</u> and the <u>avarus</u> personify the Aristotelian extremes of prodigality and meanness.

<u>virtus</u>   i.e. <u>liberalitas</u>. Cf. Hor., <u>Ep</u>. 1.18.9.

<u>medium</u>   'the mean in its relation to . . .'.

2   <u>si legisse memoras</u>   'if you recall having read . . .'.

<u>ethicam Catonis</u>   This is the so-called <u>Distycha Catonis</u>, a collection of 146 proverbs in 4 books, which though bearing the name of Cato dates to the 4th C.AD. There is a <u>praefatio</u> of pithy precepts, of which no. 7 reads: 'cum bonis ambula'. Cf. <u>Anal. Hymn.</u> 33.218.5: 'audi quid te doceat / ethica Catonis /malos vita cautius / ambula cum bonis.'.

<u>ad dandi gloriam</u>   Cf. Juv. 5.111: <u>donandi gloria</u>. Aristotle's liberal man is

concerned with being honoured (Nic. Eth. 2.7).

quis sit dignus See the preliminary comment.

3 licet Governs sis, 'though you be impartial to all in affability of face and kindly words'. For vultu hilari, cf. Cic., Tusc. 1.100.

primum videas granum, etc. 'First mark the grain among the chaff to whom you are to give . . .'. For the granum / palea image, cf. Matt. 3.12, Luke 3.17 and XIX 7 above. For videas cui des, cf. Cato, Dist. Praef. 23: 'cui des videto'.

4 non ut convenit 'inappropriately'.

non est a virtute 'is not virtuous'; a virtute is analogous with a fronte, a tergo, etc.

bonum est secundum quid, etc. 'It is good in a secondary sense, not perfectly'; the categorisation echoes such distinctions as we find in Aquinas.

intus et in cute 'inside out'; cf. Persius 3.30: 'ego te intus et in cute novi'.

5 emundas 'clear the wheat of the chaff'; cf. Columella 11.2.7 and 3 above.

largitatis oleum Cf. oleum gaudii, Isa. 61.3; oleum exultationis, Hebr. 1.9.

in te glorior The usage is both classical (Cic., N.D. 3.87, etc., but with impersonal ablative) and biblical (Isa. 49.3: 'servus meus es tu Israel, quia in te gloriabor').

Codro Codrior The name of the wretched poet who was hostile to Virgil (Ecl. 5.11, 7.22) passes into ML with the sense 'needy' or 'wretched'; cf. Latham, R.M.L.W. ad loc., and Henrici VII Ilensis, Elegia sive De Miseria (ed. Marigo, Padua 1926), 163: 'si Codrus foret hic, essem nunc Codrior illo.'.

XXIX Fortune plango vulnera

(The poem appears only in B).

This is one of a group of Fortune-poems in the C.B. (14ff.). The notion of a capricious power (Tyche/Fortuna) governing human affairs had gained strength in Hellenistic Greece and the Greek cities of the west; she was worshipped as a goddess, with temples and city-streets dedicated to her. At Rome this fickle, malevolent power was equally influential among the masses, and it is interesting to note how the great creative writers like Virgil and Livy try to reconcile Fortuna with a Stoic outlook on life; for them she personifies the operation of the World-Intelligence moving the world on its predestined course. One may see a further refinement in a writer like Apuleius, whose novel contrasts the blind Fortuna with Isis, the Fortuna with eyes; here Tyche/Fortuna, the capricious and cruel power, governs the unregenerate masses who have no eye for the true reality of the Platonist Ideas; but the initiates to the mystery-religions pass out of her control.

The goddess Fortuna continues to play a part in the cultural history of the Middle Ages, but within a Christian framework dominated by Providence. She is a symbol of the transitory nature of worldly success. She is prominent especially in the 12th Century, where "there was a strengthening of the feeling for antiquity, and an appreciation of the complexity of human history" (Raby, S.L.P. II, 261). The role of Fortuna in the careers of heroic figures like Alexander and Julius Caesar, Pompey and Cicero, was studied in romantic fiction, in the satirists, in Lucan's epic, in historiography. Perhaps the most eloquent commentary on the poems in the C.B. is the miniature of the wheel of Fortune in Benediktbeuern manuscript (see Hilka-Schumann-Bischoff, I, Tafel 1). For a general survey in English, see H.R. Patch, The Goddess Fortuna in Mediaeval Literature (Harvard 1927).

The structure of the poem is clear. Stanza 1: the nature of Fortune. Stanza 2: the poet's experience. Stanza 3: the warning to others.

1   Fortune . . . vulnera Cf. Lucan 8.72, Ovid, Pont. 2.7.41.

stillantibus ocellis So Juv. 6.109, stillantis ocelli.

rebellis 'taking up arms against me'.

fronte capillata . . . calvata As Dr. E.K. Borthwick points out to me, Philostratus (ed. Kayser II, 428) describes the Sicyon statue of Kairos by Lysippus in precisely this way. The description passes over into Latin, the immediate source of our poet being Cato, Dist. 2.26.2: 'fronte capillata, post est Occasio calva'. Hence the need to 'seize time by the forelock'.

2   <u>quicquid . . . florui . . . corrui</u>   'I have crashed from the summit of all the happiness and prosperity I enjoyed.'.

3   <u>Fortune rota</u>   A cliché in classical literature: Cic., <u>Pis</u>. 22, Tib. 1.5.70, etc.

<u>minoratus</u>   The verb is biblical; <u>Eccli</u>. 41.3, etc.

<u>nimis exaltatus</u>   So <u>Ps</u>. 96.9.

<u>vertice . . . legimus</u>   The absence of rhyme has prompted emendations; 'rex sedens in verticibus' (Herkenrath), 'rex sedet altissimus' (Lundius).

<u>Hecubam</u>   The Trojan queen often appears as an example of a monarch fallen 'beneath the wheel', because her plight was so well-known from <u>Aeneid</u> 2 and Ovid, <u>Met</u>. 13.548ff. Hence 'legimus'. Cf. <u>C.B.</u> 101.2

XXX Iste mundus furibundus

(The poem is preserved in one other ms besides B, the British Library Regius 10 D I, 14th Century).

2   campi lilia Cf. Matt. 6.28, Cant. 2.1. For their short life, cf. Hor., C. 1.36.16.

4   tartara Cf. Virg., Aen. 4.243, 6.135; Ovid, Met. 1.113, etc.

5   lex carnalis A Pauline echo; cf. Hebr. 7.16: 'legem mandati carnalis', etc.

6   fugit . . . velut umbra So Job 14.2.

7   in presenti patria Contrasted with heaven, our perennis patria; cf. Hebr. 11.16 and regularly in medieval writing.

8   quasi quercus folia Cf. Isa. 1.30: 'velut quercus defluentibus foliis . . .'.

11   conteramus, confringamus Cf. Ps. 45.10: 'arcum conteret et confringet arma'. carnis desideria Pauline; cf. Gal 5.16, etc.

12   in celesti gloria Cf. 2 Tim. 2.10.

13   gratulari mereamur The rhythm echoes the characteristic clausula of the Collects in the Roman missal.